find your voice

by Jo Thompson
& Nigel Nelson

for Rory and Louis

Artemis EDITIONS
www.artemismusic.com

First published in 2004 by

Artemis | EDITIONS

an imprint of Artemis Music Limited
Unit 3, No.3 Baring Road
Beaconsfield
Buckinghamshire
HP9 2NB

Order No. ART00029
ISBN-10: 1-904411-25-8
ISBN-13: 978-1-904411-25-3

Project editor: James Sleigh
Copy editor: Sarah Lavelle
Illustrations: Berni Georges
Front cover image: Getty Images
Back cover image: *Popstars: The Rivals* – Granada
Printed in the UK by Martins The Printers

To request a catalogue, please write to the above address or
e-mail us on info@artemismusic.com.

Artemis Editions
Made *by* musicians, *for* musicians

Discover other titles from Artemis Editions at our online shop.
Read sample chapters, view sample pages and hear MP3s at
www.artemismusicshop.com

Praise for Jo Thompson:

"Jo is a hugely talented singing coach who has encouraged me to work harder than I have ever worked before. She is a great source of inspiration." *Jane Horrocks*

"Jo has an impressive understanding of vocal technique, phrasing and style, and her great strength is her ability to apply this effectively to rock and pop singing." *Tony Hadley*

"I think our tour insurers should send Jo a huge crate of vintage champagne as without her help and advice on technique and warming up my voice, there is no way I could have completed all the shows that I've done! She really has been a great asset to me and she's a lovely person as well!" *Craig David*

"I have learned many important things from Jo. She has taught me how my body and my voice work together – her visualization techniques, for example, work unbelievably well. She has given me the confidence to relax and be natural when I perform. I think Jo was born with a gift to teach." *Ive Mendes*

"Your voice is a wonderful tool which can be massaged to perfection. Singing is healing to the body and soul. Connecting your mind and body can create some pleasantly surprising results! Thanks, Jo, for plugging me in!" *Faye Tozer*

"Jo is a great teacher. She has a way of explaining even the most difficult aspects of technique in the clearest possible ways. Working with Jo is always confidence-boosting and she has helped me find my voice, whether I'm singing West End Shows or Rock & Pop." *Lee Latchford Evans*

"When I first met Jo fourteen years ago, I was so relieved to have finally found a teacher that could relate vocal exercises and techniques to actually singing a modern pop song, plus making the process interesting and fun. We have since worked together in the studio, on film and in the classroom with great success and become life-long friends." *Kipper*

"If I had to start again, knowing what I know now, then Jo Thompson would be my first and last teacher. Probably the best vocal coach in the country." *Steve Hart*

"Jo has shown me how to be in tune with my breathing. This has helped me a huge amount, both in the studio and when singing live." *Nina Jayne*

Contents

Introduction

The last few years have seen an unprecedented interest in singing and, in particular, popular singing. As well as being an integral part of Western culture singing of all types is also now big business. With the continuing popularity of karaoke and the success of 'wannabe popstar' TV shows, more and more people want to 'have a go', many harboring aspirations to become professional singers in their own right.

Find Your Voice is an innovative and invaluable handbook for singers of any ability. It is comprehensive and user-friendly, and offers a practical, step-by-step course in singing technique, arranged in an easy-to-follow format.

Singers of all styles and at every level will learn how to:
• develop and strengthen every aspect of their singing technique
• sing with good style and phrasing
• maximize all elements of their performance
• develop auditioning skills
• take good care of their voices, and much, much more.

The teaching of singing is still largely shrouded in mystery and its history is littered with (often justified) accusations of charlatanism. Indeed, there may be people who disagree with some of the things I have to say in these pages. I make no apologies for this.

Find Your Voice is a book born of over 20 years' experience as a singing coach and represents a personal view of how things should be done: advice and tips that I have found to be helpful and important are included; advice that I think is, at best, unhelpful and at worst, downright damaging, is rejected.

It is my aim to demystify what is known about the voice and voice training, and to sort out the many myths and misunderstandings historically associated with them.

The main practical course on technique is indicated by a vertical line between the text and the edge of the page (like this paragraph), allowing the reader to view the book as a training manual. Where you are invited to try an exercise yourself, the activities suggested appear in a box.

The key components of the singing 'course', how they relate to one another, and where the relevant sections can be found in the book are given below.

A final thought. Yes, you *can* learn to be a better singer from a book – well, this book anyway. Furthermore, if you follow the basic principles and advice given within these pages, trust me, your singing could improve much more than you might have imagined – perhaps by life-changing proportions.

Good luck, and have fun!

Key Components Of The *Find Your Voice* Singing Course

Breathing (pages 12-22)

The Larynx (pages 26-28)

Singing On The Vowel (pages 80-84)

Style And Phrasing (pages 86-88)

Improvisation (pages 90-94)

Singing Exercises (pages 107-120)

Words (pages 132-135)

Visualization (pages 139-141)

Warm-Up (pages 169-172)

SECTION ONE:
HOW YOUR VOICE WORKS

Clearly, anyone can sing without knowing anything about how their voice works – singing seems to occur quite spontaneously. However, if you do know something about what is happening at a physical level, it can really help your singing. Let me explain.

We all use our voices every day in some shape or form, much in the same way that we drive our cars – automatically, or unconsciously. It is usually only when things start to go wrong that we feel the need to look below the surface.

However, good singing technique involves developing some *control* over our bodies. Take breathing. Like our heartbeat, we are hardly aware of the cycle of our breath. These things keep going – even when we are asleep.

An interesting difference between the heart and the breathing process, however, is that we can exert some control over the latter. For example, we can choose to inhale and exhale quickly or slowly, and we can even hold our breath – in other words, *stop* our breathing temporarily.

As we shall see, 'correct' breathing and **support** (see page 20) are absolutely essential to good singing. It is one of the main principles of this book that you can learn to exercise the kind of control over your breath that will greatly improve your singing. In other words, there are things to learn about the use of your breath specifically when speaking and singing that go beyond the automatic 'ebb and flow' of normal breathing.

More generally, there are many things we can learn and apply to our singing that, put together, constitute what we call **technique,** and these have their roots in the physical bits and pieces of our bodies and how we use them.

In order to understand how to sing well I believe it really helps to have some anatomical knowledge – since it provides a kind of framework or skeleton on which you can hang everything else you learn about your singing.

So, although the thought of a quick biology lesson might switch some of you off (my editor, in fact, admitted to being a little squeamish about talk of lungs, larynx, diaphragm and the like, but I told him to pull himself together), I suggest that if you take the trouble to read this section, everything that follows will make a lot more sense. In addition, there are a number of exercises I recommend here that will help you get in touch with the parts of your body you should be using when you sing.

The first two chapters in this section, *Breath* and *Vocal Cords,* deal with how the basic singing sound is produced and, from the singer's point of view, the most effective way to go about this. The key concept of *support* is discussed here. There then follows a chapter on the *Larynx,* and one on *The Mouth,* in which the importance of the tongue, jaw, soft palate and pharynx is explained.

Finally, there are places in this book that deal specifically with voice problems. If you know a little about what can go wrong physically, it can be a lot easier to put things right, or, better still, avoid having problems in the first place.

So here goes – let's get physical!

Chapter 1
Breath

Without breath – well, let's face it, you wouldn't be reading this now! Seriously though, breathing properly and supporting the breath correctly is the key to singing well. Without air the sound would not happen. Let's start by looking closely at what happens to the breath and how the sound is created.

The Cycle Of Breath

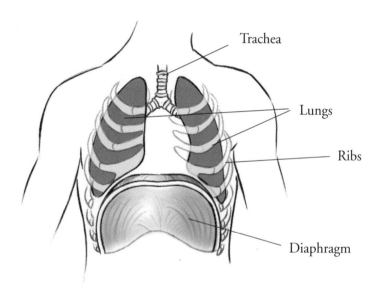

Trachea

Lungs

Ribs

Diaphragm

Breathing In

As you breathe in, air travels in through your nose or mouth, through your larynx (voice box), down your trachea (windpipe) and into your lungs. Your lungs and the ribcage that surrounds them expand – you can imagine yourself as a big balloon filling with air.

Breathing Out

As you breathe out, the air flows out of your lungs, back up through your trachea, through your larynx and out of your nose or mouth.

It is when the air is flowing back through your larynx that the sound is made. Your vocal cords (or vocal *folds*) are inside this 'box' and as the air, under pressure, passes over them they vibrate and it is this that creates the sound. (See *Vocal Cords,* page 23)

The Diaphragm

The diaphragm is a big, strong, dome-shaped muscle that separates your heart and lungs from the rest of your insides. It is the main muscle involved in breathing. The diaphragm is joined to your sternum (breastbone) at the front and to your spine at the back. The diaphragm works like a bellows – the rise-and-fall motion of the diaphragm fills and empties air from the lungs.

As you breathe in, your diaphragm flattens out. As it does so it squashes down onto your other organs and pushes your abdomen out. As you breathe out it moves back up.

Thorax area
(including the heart and lungs)

Diaphragm

Abdominal area
(including other
internal organs)

Gaining Control Over Your Breathing

To start to develop any control over your singing you have to get to grips with your breathing. You need to develop an understanding and awareness of your breathing: how it feels to breathe deeply, and how it feels to control this deep breath in the most effective way.

To achieve a smooth, flowing sound you need smooth-flowing breath. You have to be able to control the out-flow of air as you are singing and not lose it all in one go. You must learn how to release the breath gradually, thereby keeping it 'available' for controlling the sound (and to be able to sustain any length of phrase). This control of the breath is known as **support**, which we shall be looking at in detail later.

You might think there is only one way of breathing, but you can in fact breathe in different ways. These methods can be categorized as *clavicular*, *intercostal* and *diaphragmatic*. As I will explain, *diaphragmatic* breathing is the type of breathing you should be developing – the other two should be avoided. Let me explain why.

Clavicular Breathing

This means breathing into your clavicles, which sounds quite nasty doesn't it? Actually, clavicles are another word for your collarbones. When breathing predominantly in this way you will feel you are breathing high up in your chest. If you direct the breath here, around the top of your lungs, it will be shallow and will feel 'snatched' or 'gasped'. You will also feel tight across your chest and shoulders and this will be reflected in your singing. Incidentally, this is where you breathe when you are in panic mode. So, clearly, if you are feeling anxious when you sing, you can get into a vicious circle of constantly snatching in breath, which in turn fuels the feeling of panic. In brief – don't do it!

Breathing in this way is a common problem for untrained singers. If the breath is too 'high' it won't be possible to have any real control over your singing. You will never be able to sing long phrases or hold notes. Remember, it is the breath that makes the sound happen.

Intercostal Breathing

The ribcage houses the lungs and consists of twelve pairs of ribs. All of them can move, except for the first pair. The intercostal muscles connect the ribs to each other. As you breathe in the external intercostals lift the ribs and allow more space for your lungs to fill with air. As you breathe out the internal intercostals pull the ribs back down.

Some singing teachers focus primarily on this way of breathing. It is certainly true that the intercostals play a part in controlling the diaphragm as you breathe out, but I don't like focusing on the breath here. I was taught this technique and encouraged to practice singing with my hands on the sides of my ribcage. This technique works for some people, but it created a huge amount of tension in my body and therefore my singing, so I am not going to recommend it to you.

Diaphragmatic Breathing

Now you're talking! The diaphragm is the most active and important muscle involved in breathing. The fall-and-rise action of the diaphragm fills and empties air from the lungs. As you breathe out, the diaphragm is controlled by a combination of the abdominal (abs) and intercostal muscles. The abdominal muscles have most control and are very active when you speak and sing. I prefer to concentrate on using my abdominal muscles when I sing.

Here is a good exercise to help you feel those abs working. If you do the exercise correctly you will begin to understand what I mean by diaphragmatic breathing.

Stand with your feet the width of your hips apart. Put your hands on your tummy, just above your tummy button. Breathe in and out slowly through your nose. As you breathe in you should feel your tummy moving out; as you breathe out feel your tummy come back in. Breathe in again and this time let the air out in short bursts making a 'ss' sound. Your tummy should feel like it is 'springing' in with each out-breath.

Note: Dancers have been trained to pull their tummies in as they breathe in. They therefore, find it difficult to adjust to the idea that when you breathe in to sing, your tummy should move out.

The muscles that you feel working in this exercise are the ones you should use to control your breath while singing. They need to be permanently 'switched on', but there are times when you will have to use them more. For example, when you sing a high or sustained note you need greater control over your breath, so you increase the muscle tension. This is at the root of what we call **support** (see page 20) which I will move on to after we have done some work on our breathing.

Incidentally, when I talk about the tummy I mean the area just above your tummy button. Focusing on the breath in this area enables you to relax the rest of your body. If you think of the breath too low down, this can restrict the free movement of your ribcage.

> *Place both hands on your abdomen – one above your tummy button and one below. As you breathe in, the lower hand should stay still and the upper hand should move outwards. As you sing, try to get the breath working in this way – it will help you gain full control over your diaphragm.*

The more you practice controlling your breath in the right way, the more natural it will feel and the easier your singing will become. When you are supporting your voice well, you will feel the muscles in your lower back beginning to work. This will happen naturally. Don't try to force them to work as it can create tension in your breath and body.

Don't adopt any breathing practices that feel awkward or uncomfortable. Trust your natural instinct. If something doesn't feel good don't do it!

Mental Control

Because you can't see or really imagine what is happening to the muscles involved, you need to develop some mental imagery that helps you to achieve or 'anchor' the kind of control you need. For example, I never think of pushing *out* sound or breath; instead I think about drawing it *in* (where I gain control of it). By thinking about it – directing your thoughts into particular areas – you can alter the places where you feel the breath and where the sound resonates.

Breathing Exercises

Some voice teachers are not big fans of breathing exercises but I think they are essential for getting in touch with your breathing, feeling its natural rhythm, and experiencing its full potential.

Most of my examples are based on Hatha yoga breathing practices. There are many different ones: you may have heard of the exercise that involves holding a candle in front of your mouth and breathing out slowly and steadily, whilst trying not to blow out the flame. I have included my favorites here, none of which, incidentally, involves any fire risk.

Breathing exercises are also brilliant for relaxation. I use them a lot to help singers steady their nerves before a live gig or TV performance. Many performers (and sportsmen and women) feel terrible before they go out to perform – a mixture of nerves and excess adrenalin – and some are physically sick. Apart from their other obvious uses, then, breathing exercises can make pre-concert dressing rooms more pleasant places to be!

Exercises

1. Three-stage Breathing

I love this yoga breathing exercise. It is incredibly relaxing and it reaches parts of your lungs that other exercises just don't reach!

Lie on the floor with your knees bent and your feet flat on the floor, with your head resting on two medium-sized paperbacks. Rest your hands on your tummy, around the tummy button area. Breathe in and out through your nose. Relax and consciously slow down your breathing. Picture the bottom of your lungs filling with air as you breathe in. If your mind starts to wander bring it back to your breathing. Do this for a few minutes.

Next, move your hands onto the middle of your tummy. Picture the middle of your lungs filling with air and feel your ribcage at the front, sides and back moving in to the floor. Again, do this for a few minutes.

Now place your hands on top of your chest. Breathe in to your collarbones. Use the in-breath to help you open up across your chest. Use the out-breath, which is the relaxing breath, to let go of tension. I like this bit. As singers we are always trying to avoid breathing here but it feels good to open up this area.

Finally, place your hands back on your lower tummy and breathe using the whole of your lungs. As you breathe in, picture filling your lungs from the bottom up, and as you breathe out empty them from the top down.

I do this exercise most nights before going to sleep – it makes your back feel great and helps to clear your mind of any stresses you have from the day. Doing this exercise every night might not be such a good idea if you have recently started a new relationship!

2. Counting Breath

This exercise has a calming effect, leaving your mind and body feeling 'quiet'. Use the thought of breath being 'quiet' to help you avoid gasping in air just before you sing.

Part 1: Lie on the floor as in exercise 1. Slowly breathe in through your nose. Note that in all these exercises so far you have been breathing in through your nose – not your mouth. Breathing through your nose is more relaxing and it is easier to get the breath into the bottom of your lungs. When you sing you have to take the air in through your mouth as there isn't time to breathe in through your nose.

Breathe in and out slowly, making your in-breath and out-breath the same length. Go with the natural rhythm of your breath.

Part 2: Repeat Part 1. Breathe in, hold the breath for the same count, and then breathe out for the same count.

Part 3: Repeat part 2, but this time, after you have breathed out, pause for the same count and then breathe in again. So the pattern is: breathe in, pause, breathe out, pause – don't strain. If it feels too much for you, stop.

3. Humming-bee Breath

This exercise is good for observing the steadiness of your airflow.

Sit or kneel comfortably. Hum a note (not too high) on an 'mmm' sound, with your lips lightly touching. You should feel the note vibrating around your nose and the front of your face, or in your chest (or a bit of both). The sound will resemble that of a buzzing bee.

Notice how long the breath lasts. Is it shaky? Does it come in waves? With practice you can make the sound even. To start with, try practicing for two minutes and gradually increase it to five minutes. You can try varying the pitch of the note – take it a little higher or lower. If you practice this in a group you can get some amazing harmonies and clusters of sound going.

This is also incredibly relaxing – both for the voice and mind.

4. Getting In Touch With Your Diaphragm

I use this exercise to wake up my diaphragm.

You can do this exercise standing, kneeling or sitting (either cross-legged or on a chair). If standing, have your feet the width of your hips apart. Spread your bodyweight evenly. Put your hands low down onto your tummy. Breathe out hard through your nose – it sounds like a reversed sniff. Let the air spring straight back in through your nose. The emphasis is on the out-breath – the in-breath will happen spontaneously. Do this 10 times, about one breath every second. Then take a few normal breaths. When you feel ready repeat the exercise. If you are going dizzy, stop – you've been taking in too much oxygen. If you feel you can manage it, try it a third time, but with your hands by your sides. Build up to 30 in one go.

At the end of this exercise your breath should feel considerably more relaxed and lower in your body. I love the feeling of the power of my diaphragm. As you breathe out you can feel it coming up strongly. It's a bit like a taut trampoline. If you can feel your diaphragm working in this way you are well on your way to understanding **support.**

Breathing For Singing

Working on the exercises will give you a feel for how you should be breathing when you sing: avoid snatching or gasping air in; keep your chest and shoulders relaxed; keep the breath low and let it flow smoothly.

It is when you come to sing, however, that things can go a bit pear-shaped. You might start out okay but the more you sing, the harder you may find it to keep your breath low enough. If this is happening, your breath is *clavicular* (see page 14) – you are gasping air in a shallow way. As we have seen, you need to anchor the breath around your 'middle' and feel the support through the control of your diaphragm. (You will find more about how to use your breath specifically when singing a song in the *Breathing Within A Song* section on page 83)

Having identified the correct way of breathing, it is now time to look more closely at *how* to control the breath when singing. This vitally important control of the breath is known as *Support.*

Support

Nearly every singer or singing teacher will give you a different description of what support is and how to achieve it. However, everyone is agreed that it is about the control of air as you sing and is absolutely fundamental to any singing technique. Without control of the breath you won't have control over length of phrase, tone, resonance, range, dynamics – the lot!

There are two main schools of thought. In the first, the one I go for, singers work to 'slow down' or control the *inward* movement of their abdominal muscles as they breathe out (which, of course, thereby controls the movement of the diaphragm). Remember, as you breathe in, your diaphragm flattens out and your abdominal muscles move out. As you breathe out, your diaphragm comes back up and your abdominal muscles move back in. The thing I particularly like about this method is that the control is very much in tune with the way your breathing system naturally works.

In the second, singers 'push out' as they breathe out – the aim being to resist the upward movement of the diaphragm. This way of supporting tends to be more of a male thing as it is very physical (although some women do practice it). You need a lot of strength to keep this going. I was taught a version of this method and it didn't work for me. In fact it resulted in me singing with a huge amount of tension in my body.

In my experience, if you do 'push out' it is very easy to put pressure on your vocal cords and strain your voice – as well as over-tensing your body. It seems to me that you are working too much against nature. After all, the natural way is for your tummy or abdomen to come in as you breathe out. I would emphasize that the method of support *I* am recommending works equally well for men and women.

There should be no squeezing or forcing when you control the breath. The control should be experienced as a subtle form of sustained muscular tension in the abdominal muscles as you breathe out, but not a rigid one. However, when you start a phrase you need to engage the muscles so that they are ready to work. This could be described as a 'pull in'. If you do the following exercise you will know what this feels like.

Support can also be thought of as controlling a *springiness* in the abdominal muscles as you breathe out. Once you have pulled your abdominal muscles in, you need to continue to exert control over them otherwise you will lose control of the breath. You should support the beginning of every phrase and continue this support evenly throughout.

To check this out, repeat the exercise on page 15 (in the section on diaphragmatic breathing), putting your hands on your tummy, breathing out on a 'sss' sound. With each 'sss' your tummy should 'spring' in. It does this naturally as a result of the air coming out. This is what it feels like when you support your voice.

When you are singing and supporting the sound, you consciously have to make this 'spring' happen.

Now repeat the exercise, letting the breath out as slowly as you can. The more slowly you let the breath out, the more you will feel the muscle tension. It is this kind of sustained tension you should be feeling when you are supporting your singing.

There are times, however, when you will need a bit of extra support – for example, if you are singing long or high notes or a sustained phrase. Here I would make my abdominal muscles work harder and draw more strength from them. It is all about having a high degree of control over the airflow. Don't pull the muscles too hard though, as you can put too much pressure on your vocal cords – you could also push all the air out in one go! As a general rule, I don't like any 'techniques' that involve too much squeezing, pulling, pushing, etc.

In order to visualize support, you may find it helpful to think of an inflated balloon in your stomach from which you very gradually let out air as you sing.

There is another crucial element to support. This is the role of the **larynx**. It is very important that when you sing you keep a low, relaxed larynx. This does not mean that you forcibly push your larynx down. Again, this is achieved by mental control.

In my view, support is achieved through working the muscles that control the breath in the way I have described, whilst simultaneously maintaining a 'low' larynx (see *Keeping A Low Larynx,* page 27).

To help you achieve this, visualize having a big round tube that reaches from the back of your throat right down into your body. Think of your larynx as a weight that 'leans' down into this space. Try to imagine pushing a beach ball under water as you sing. If you push the ball down the buoyancy of the air inside it will push it back up again and the ball will come out of the water. You have to keep pushing the ball (or the sound) down against the diaphragm, which is coming up. It is a feeling of compression.

I also think of a large platform (my diaphragm), low down in my tummy, that the sound 'cruises' on as I sing.

When you have both elements working together, the feeling is one of your whole body being involved in making the sound, and the results are exhilarating!

Chapter 2
The Vocal Cords

What Are They?

Let's get something right first: you spell them cords (as in rope), not chords (as in a group of musical notes). They are also referred to as the vocal folds, or 'true' vocal folds. This is the term used by doctors and speech therapists and is a better description of what they really are.

People have all sorts of strange ideas about what the vocal cords look like and how many there are. Well, each of us has just two of them and they reach from the front to the back of the larynx or voice box (see diagram below). They are attached to the thyroid cartilage, the front of which is called the Adam's Apple. This 'thyroid cartilage' is hard and protects the cords.

The cords lie stretched across the top of the trachea and, as the air passes out through the lungs, it passes over the cords (which have been drawn together); they vibrate and the sound is produced. Think how you can make a squealing noise by blowing through two blades of grass held together between your thumbs – it is a similar process.

Vocal cords in repose

Vocal cords
(true vocal folds)

Trachea

Ventricular fold
(false vocal fold)

Vocal cords in the production of sound

Note: There is, in fact, another pair of cords called the 'false' vocal cords (or folds). They lie above and parallel to the true cords. They help to protect the vocal cords and when you swallow they come together to make a firm valve or seal. They shouldn't really be involved in making sound but for some people with voice problems they do come into play – resulting in a low, muffled, throaty sound.

Incidentally, in the eighteenth century Antoine Ferrein, one of the first people to study vocal physiology conducted an experiment to see how the larynx produced sound. His experiment involved using the larynx of a dead dog. He pulled the vocal cords together and blew into the trachea and to his delight a sound was produced. I mention this only to remind us that, with the help of this book, there is now no excuse for singing like a dog!

KEY POINT

The actual singing sound is created by the vocal cords or folds, which vibrate as the out-breath passes over them.

Your vocal cords are highly elastic and have a very complex structure, being made up of lots of different types of tissue and muscle fibers. They are always closed at the front and open like a 'V' at the back.

When you are not making any sound, your vocal cords are quite slack. The opening between the cords is called the 'chink of the glottis'. When you sing the cords are brought close together and the 'chink' disappears. Depending on how low or high you are singing, more or less of the cords vibrate. When you sing a low note the cords are pulled together and the whole mass vibrates.

Gradually, as you sing higher, the 'tension' on your cords is increased as they are pulled more taut and, as a result, less of the cords vibrate. When you sing a high note, only the inside edges of the cords are vibrating. Think how the pitch of a guitar string is altered. You raise the pitch by tightening it and lower the pitch by slackening it off.

Remember, this is only the start. Once the sound is produced it is what you *do* with it that is important and defines the kind of singer you will be. There is in fact a huge amount you *can* do with the raw sound and this will all be covered in Section Three.

Problems With Your Cords

There are various nasty things that can develop on and around your cords if you don't look after them: nodules, cysts, polyps and burst blood vessels. Other than straining your voice when you sing incorrectly, the commonest cause of voice strain is excessive shouting – whether it be at football games, concerts, over-loud music or during post-gig socializing!

Heavy voice use at work can also be damaging – many schoolteachers, for example, have real problems. If you have a cough or throat infection, persistent voice use can also cause damage. For more information on these kinds of problems and what to do about them, read the section *Maintenance, Breakdown And Recovery*, page 155.

Chapter 3
The Larynx

The larynx, or voice box, is situated at the top of the trachea (windpipe) and below the pharynx (back wall of the throat). It is a kind of V-shaped box made of cartilage, joined together by ligaments, membranes and muscles, and it contains the vocal cords. The sharp end of it points forward and sticks out in the throat.

It feels a bit odd, and some people can't stand doing this, but you can actually move your larynx around.

Put one hand on either side of your neck, in line with your Adam's Apple and gently move your larynx from side to side. It feels quite strange, as it is suspended from your hyoid or tongue bone.

The larynx is very important to us and does a number of jobs. At the top of it, at the back, is your epiglottis. This is a 'flap' of cartilage that closes off the larynx when you are drinking and eating and stops you choking. It also acts as an air passage as well as housing your vocal cords.

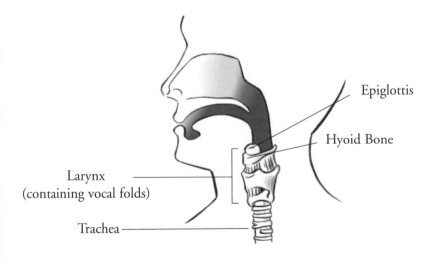

Epiglottis

Hyoid Bone

Larynx
(containing vocal folds)

Trachea

The larynx is incredibly muscular. Some muscles lift the larynx and some lower it. The sternocleidomastoids (phew!) are some that we don't want to see in action at all. These are the big ones at the side of the neck that stand out when singers are straining. Invariably, these people will be singing with an extremely high larynx.

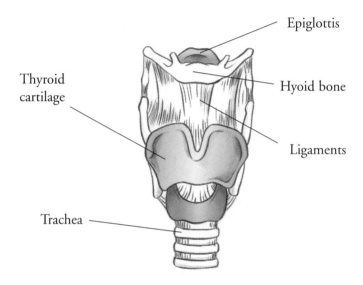

Epiglottis

Thyroid cartilage

Hyoid bone

Ligaments

Trachea

What happens when you sing high notes?

Rest your hands gently on your larynx. Sing a low note and join it to a high note. Does your larynx move up? I think you'll find it does.

Keeping A Low Larynx

Many singers experience tightness in their throats as they sing high notes. Well, as I have mentioned, some of the muscles inside your larynx will help you to keep it low and relaxed. The thing about these muscles is that you can't grab hold of them to feel them working; you get them to do what you want through mental control.

It is easy really. Every time you sing higher, think 'down' (but don't reverse it and think 'up' as you sing down). As you sing, use mental pictures to help you: think of an elevator plunging down in its shaft; a cafetière being pushed down; a see-saw going down as the singing comes up. One or more of these images will work very powerfully for you – you will be very surprised what a difference they can make in freeing the sound you produce.

KEY POINT

It is essential to keep a 'low larynx' when singing. This is achieved by using mental imagery and control.

Never try to force your larynx down – that will create tension. Avoid pushing down with the back of your tongue. The idea is to keep your larynx in a relaxed position while singing.

This technique really does work. A well-known singer I work with said it has completely transformed her singing. She now no longer worries about singing high notes whilst performing.

As I mentioned before, it is the combination of the low, relaxed larynx working with your controlled breath that will give you a properly supported voice when you sing.

*Note: **Appoggiare la Voce** is an Italian expression meaning 'to lean on the voice', and is the term classical singers use when referring to singing with a low larynx.*

Chapter 4
The Mouth And Jaw

The sound obviously comes out of your mouth when you sing, however, its main function is not to act as a resonator. We use it primarily to shape the vowel sounds, and the lips, teeth and tongue all work together to articulate the consonants. If you have tension in any of these areas it can tie up your singing. The jaw and tongue are prime examples.

The Jaw And Tongue

It is very important to keep a relaxed jaw and tongue when you sing. They are interconnected with your larynx so if there are unwanted tensions here, these will directly and adversely affect your singing.

Many singers find that their jaws become very tight and tense and their tongues ache when they sing. These are probably the most common areas of tension amongst singers.

The tongue is connected to the larynx via the hyoid, or tongue bone (see diagram, page 30), which is a lot larger than you might think. Only the tip of it is visible in your mouth; most of it lies in your throat. When you sing, your tongue should lie flat in your mouth. Obviously when you sing words the tip has to come forward to help with consonants such as t, s and l, but you should still keep your tongue as relaxed as possible at all times.

Some voice teachers make you do weird things with your tongue such as getting you to lift it high at the back – a 'technique' I was forced to suffer. Avoid anything unnatural. Try not to press it down at the back. Some people do this in an effort to keep a low larynx. You will experience an ache around the base of your tongue. Watch out for it.

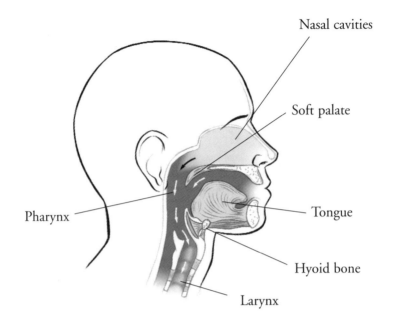

It is harder to keep your tongue relaxed when singing certain vowels. We are all different in terms of our accents and mouth and throat shapes. As a result of this we vary in the way we find certain vowels more difficult to sing than others.

'Ee', for example, can be a tricky vowel sound for some people – it can make you pull your tongue up. 'Oo' can make you pull your tongue forward. 'Oh', 'awe' and 'ah' can also cause problems – some people will push down at the back of the tongue or tense the base of the tongue as they sing higher. In addition, many singers tense and almost lock their jaws on 'ah'.

Identifying where you have tension is the first step towards getting rid of it. With practice you can then learn to let go of these tensions and free up your singing.

The Jaw

Most of us hold a huge amount of tension in our jaws. In the Far East there is a practice of jaw massage. Apparently, after one of these you can feel amazing. But I read somewhere that the pain you experience having the massage is close to that of childbirth! (I don't think it likely – probably written by a man!)

Joking apart, it is vital to have a loose, free jaw when you sing. It should hinge open and never come forward. Your chin should move back and down. If it comes forward, you will put pressure on your larynx and tighten up your singing.

In The Groove

I love this! There is a groove that you can feel through your cheeks between your upper and lower teeth, at the back. It feels like a small cavity on either side of your cheeks. Try to find it.

> *Place your index fingers in the grooves. Open and close your mouth. You can feel the movement of your jaw - how you can swing it forwards or back. It feels amazing singing like this. It gives you real freedom. Try singing a song with your fingers in this position. Note how much you want to bring your jaw forward and how easy it is to sing if you don't.*

I think of this as my 'get out of jail free card'. If you have problems with a song this will help you to place it correctly.

Many singers tighten their jaws if they push their chest voice too high. As they drive the sound up, their chins and jaws tighten with it. You need to allow head resonance to 'mix' with the sound as you sing higher (see *Registers,* page 61).

Don't underestimate how bad a tight jaw can get. One person I used to teach had the most extreme jaw tension I have ever come across. She was doing a lot of singing on a course where the voice teachers were inexperienced and had very little knowledge of technique. She was a jaw-clencher, caused by a problem unrelated to singing. When she sang, her jaw went into spasm and completely locked. It became so bad that her whole face swelled up and she could not move her mouth at all. She saw a specialist and was advised not to speak for a month. After her lay-off she had to start from scratch with her singing technique, but it was a real challenge for her.

The Mouth

Don't confuse singing with a visit to the dentist. When you are singing, you really don't need to 'open wide'. Again, this was one of the techniques I was taught that introduced more tension into my singing than anything else.

It is true that as you sing higher you need to open your mouth more, but if it is wide when you are singing low, where have you to go? It was a total revelation when I discovered that, certainly in the middle and lower registers of your voice, you don't need to open your mouth very wide at all. It is much easier to control the sound and keep it focused if you don't.

If your mouth is wide open, too much air pours out and the sound loses its direction. It makes it much more difficult to control the ends of phrases and it can often sound like the singing has 'collapsed', with the tone petering out.

This mouth position is widely used, particularly in classical music and 'open-throated' singing. While I am a fan of singing with a nice open space at the back of the throat, you don't need a wide-open mouth to achieve this (see *Open throat,* page 55). Also, if your mouth position is too wide in the lower registers, as you sing higher it becomes very difficult not to tense your jaw or bring it forward.

The Soft Palate

If you run a finger over the roof of your mouth at the back you will feel a soft, squidgy bit. This is the soft palate. The small pointy bit that hangs down is called the uvula and this has a muscle in it that allows you to draw it up and back. Some people confuse this with their tonsils and others even their vocal cords!

The soft palate needs to be lifted as you sing higher to allow the sound to move into the correct position (see *Registers*, page 61). If you don't lift it, the sound will stay too dark and will feel squashed inside. The best thing to imagine is an 'inner smile' gradually increasing as you go higher. Some people think of it as a yawn. I was taught at one time to sing with a massive cheesy grin on my face – even to sing and brush my teeth at the same time. It might feel quite good for your jaw, but not only do you look like a complete idiot when you sing, the sound loses all focus and becomes woolly.

The Pharynx

This is the name given to the area at the back of the throat. The back wall contains a lot of muscles and these can alter its shape and size. It is a very important resonator (see page 51) and when you sing, this area should feel open and not squashed or restricted in any way.

SECTION ONE SUMMARY

- It is not necessary to know anything about how your voice works in order to sing, but some knowledge of the physical processes involved will greatly help your understanding and development of technique.

- Although breathing is an automatic process, you can exert some control over it. You can learn to use the muscles involved in breathing and in other parts of your body in ways that will maximize your ability to sing.

- To develop any control over your singing, you need to control the flow of air as you sing.

- The control of breath is known as **support**.

- Controlling the flow of breath with your **diaphragm** is the key to support.

- Correct support is achieved by combining control of the out-breath with a **low larynx**.

- Performing the exercises recommended in this section will help you:
    a) to get in touch with your breathing
    b) to become aware of the muscles involved in support
    c) to strengthen the support mechanism
    d) to maintain a low larynx when singing.

- A great deal of singing technique is learned through the use of mental control and imagery.

- Unwanted tensions in the tongue and jaw can adversely affect your singing.

- The **soft palate** needs to be 'lifted' as you sing higher.

SECTION TWO:
BODY TALK

In Section One we learned that the best way to produce and control the basic singing sound is by breathing properly, supporting the breath and keeping a low larynx. We also saw how unwanted tension in the jaw and tongue can hinder our singing.

But singing involves your *whole* body and how you use the other areas of your body is also very important. If you have unwanted tension in virtually *any* part of your body, it can affect the way the sound is produced.

If you have a tense body, this tension will be transferred to your singing. Equally, if your body is relaxed, open and free, this will be strongly reflected in your voice.

In this section I will discuss the importance of keeping your body *open, wide and free*, and describe how to achieve this. We shall consider the particular challenges facing singers who also play instruments, since good body use for these people can sometimes be more difficult to achieve.

At the end of the section I shall briefly describe how such practices as Alexander Technique and Yoga can be particularly helpful to the singer, and I have included in this section some exercises of my own designed to free up your body.

Note: In Section Three we shall look at the key concept of *resonance* – the way we use areas in our body to *resonate* the sound in order to amplify and add color to it.

Chapter 5
Open, Wide And Free

A Free Body

The importance of having a free body when singing cannot be underestimated. As we have seen, tension not only in the jaw and tongue, but also in other areas of your body can significantly and detrimentally affect your singing.

In terms of body use I have a mantra for all singers:

WHEN YOU SING YOU SHOULD BE **OPEN**, **WIDE** AND **FREE**.

Let me explain. What happens when we sing with a free body? Have you noticed, for example, how well you sing in the bath or shower? It is partly the acoustic that helps, of course, but our bodies are also invariably very relaxed and tension-free at these times. Our voices can flow through our bodies and fill the bathroom with sound. It's never the same if you think someone is listening, because you immediately tense up!

The ways in which singers perform live vary considerably. Some singers are quite static when they perform; others throw themselves around dramatically. A very physical performance can add to the general excitement, but you may fear that the singing will inevitably suffer. However, the opposite is usually the case. Many singers achieve an open and freer body this way, which in turn liberates their voices.

Whatever you do with your body has a direct result on the sound that you produce. Let's see how we can open up our bodies in a helpful way, and what we can do to avoid unwanted tension.

Standing

Ideally, when you are singing, you should stand with your feet the width of your hips apart. Your head should be balanced, shoulders relaxed, and your chest open, but not pushed forward. Make sure you are not tensing your legs or your bottom. Your body should feel relaxed, balanced and open. Try to maintain this posture when singing.

Even when you are not standing still, try to keep these principles of good body use in mind. The more demanding the singing, the more attention you should give to the way you use your body.

Ideally you should experience a 'free' body not only when standing, but also when sitting and singing, playing any instrument, or moving around the stage.

The Head

You will have seen many singers pulling their heads back in an attempt to hit the high notes or pushing them down to reach the low notes. Psychologically you may feel that it helps you to do this, as people generally associate singing high with reaching, and singing low with pushing down. Throwing your head around in this way might look dramatic; however it is not at all helpful.

Don't pull your head back or push it down as this will not only put pressure on your larynx, it will also affect the connection with your breath. If you consider what's happening physically, the air doesn't have a free passage to your vocal cords. Keep the back of your neck long at all times. Incidentally, also be careful when singing with a microphone – make sure the stand is not too high or low for the same reasons.

Put one hand on the back of your neck. Pull your head back. You can feel it squashing the back of your neck. As you do this you also collapse forward across your chest and shoulders.

Body Tension

Legs And Bottom

Don't tense these. If you do, it will be hard to keep your breath relaxed and low. It will also make you tense your back and shoulders.

Shoulders

Keep these relaxed. Don't hold them up by your ears, keep them opening back and down into your shoulder blades. Don't push them forward. If you tense your shoulders it will inhibit the free flow of your breath and tighten up your singing.

Arms

Relax your arms and hands. If you clench your fists you automatically clench other parts of your body. Tense arms and clenched fists will, for example, restrict the freedom of your breathing

Occupational Hazards

It is not only what you are doing when you are singing that can cause you problems. How you use yourself in everyday life, particularly at work, can throw your body out of line. Take, for example, being slumped over a keyboard or staring at a computer screen for much of the day. It really is very difficult in these situations not to collapse your body and to stay open across your chest.

We can build up so many tensions without even being aware of them – consider all the RSI sufferers there are – that it then becomes very difficult to leave these tensions behind when we start singing. I know there are a lot of things to think about all at the same time, but once you adopt certain habits, good body use will soon become second nature.

Here is a series of exercises that will make you more aware of your body and what you are doing with it when you sing. If you practice these you will gain more freedom in your body and therefore in your singing.

Exercises To Free Up Your Body

The position for this exercise is the same as for three-stage breathing (see page 17). In this exercise you are not only concentrating on the breath but on 'letting go' of tension in your body.

Lie on the floor on your back with your head resting on two average-sized paperbacks (this supports your head and ensures you're not scrunching up the back of your neck). Bend your knees, keeping your feet flat on the floor, and rest your hands on your tummy. Breathe in and out through your nose slowly and deeply.

Concentrate on your back spreading into the floor, feel your ribcage and shoulders opening out onto the floor. Think about your chest getting wider and your body longer. Try to let go of your neck (remember the weight of your head is being supported by the books).

Lie here for at least ten minutes – the longer the better. It feels fantastic! This will not only relax you and get you more in touch with your breathing, it will help you open up across your chest and shoulders, and make you feel more 'open' in your body for singing.

The following exercise gives your back a lovely twist, and opens you out across your chest.

Lie on the floor as above. You may want to try this without the books, it's up to you – whatever feels best for your neck. Stretch your arms out to the sides of your body, palms facing upwards. Keeping your knees together and feet on the floor, breathe out and rotate your knees over to one side. You may find it feels good to turn your head the opposite way. Stay here for a few minutes (if it doesn't feel comfortable, come up, breathing slowly). When you have had enough, breathe in and bring your knees back to the middle. Breathe out and rotate your knees over to the other side, turning your head the opposite way. Make sure that your shoulders are in contact with the floor – if not you should stretch your legs out more or lower your arms slightly.

If it feels very easy, you can repeat the twist starting with your knees over your chest and feet off the floor. Be careful not to put any strain on your back. If you feel it pulling, put your feet back on the floor.

Exercises While You Sing

When I introduce these exercises to people they often ask whether I have a hidden camera in the room for blackmail purposes. They are fun and sound a bit strange initially, but all serve a serious purpose so please try them!

While you sing, hold a plant pot or large glass on your head. Don't worry, you haven't got to balance the object. Hold it with both hands, keeping your chest open and elbows pointing out to the walls. Not only will you feel that it's easier to breathe, but your head will be balanced and your body open and stretched. It is all well and good to tell people not to pull back their heads when they sing, but singers who do this have often developed a very strong habit that is hard to break. This exercise reinforces the feeling of singing with a well-balanced head.

This next exercise gives you a great stretch and opens you up across your chest and shoulders as you sing.

Stand up straight and take the thumb of your right hand over your right shoulder, as if you were hitchhiking. Next, stretch the arm out as far as you can to the side, pointing your fingers. Put these two things together in one smooth sequence. Hold the stretch. Take your arm down and repeat on the other side.

If you only stretched your arm out without the 'hitching' movement, it would not be as effective. This is because the 'hitching' rotates your shoulder outwards and therefore opens out your chest more.

Now sing and do the exercise. Every time you take a breath, swap sides. It takes a bit of practice to co-ordinate everything, but it's well worth it.

Another simple thing to try is to let your arms hang loosely by your sides, and then swing them backwards and forwards as you sing. This will liberate your singing as it helps to loosen you up.

Walking rhythmically (and marching) as you sing is very helpful. Singers often find that they build up tension if they are standing still and concentrating. Swinging your arms while walking is even better for freeing you up.

Singing and scrubbing your back is another great thing to try. Imagine you are scrubbing your back from above with a long brush. Have a good brush one side and then change arms. This helps to open you up across your chest.

Whilst singing, rub your back with a towel. Hold it with both hands and move it up and down diagonally across your back. When you have had enough change sides. Again, this opens you up across your chest.

A balance board is great to use if you have one. Mine is a piece of wood about 2 cm (3/4") thick, 85 cm (35") long and 38 cm (15") wide, balanced on a wooden roller about 10 cm (4") in diameter. The idea is to sing and balance at the same time. Apart from being great fun, the balance board helps you to keep your legs, bottom and hips free, as well as keeping a balanced head when you sing. If you tense up anywhere you will fall off!

Chapter 6
Singing With An Instrument

There are many examples of great singers who also play an instrument. In fact, their playing often complements and enhances their singing performance.

There are, however, some problems to overcome when both singing and playing. It is easy to find yourself falling into bad ways of using your body – doing those things, in other words, that prevent you from maintaining a body that is open, wide and free.

The Pianist

When singing and playing, keep open across your chest. Don't lift your shoulders; keep them relaxed. Make sure that your elbows aren't stuck to your sides. Don't hunch over the piano as this will restrict the space for your breath and make it hard to sing long phrases or have any volume.

Keep your head balanced. It is tempting to pull it back, leaving you with a lifted chin and shortened back of the neck (this will put pressure on your larynx and stop your voice from being connected to your breath).

Don't wobble your head around either – you will lose stability in your voice and connection with the breath. We have all seen famous artists break these rules, but trust me: it's better for your singing if you don't!

If you are using a microphone at the piano, be careful about its position. Make sure you don't have to lean forward or pull your head too far up or down to reach the mic. If the mic position is awkward you may find yourself compromising the balance of your head or closing across your chest and shoulders. As a result the singing will be restricted. Be careful to keep the length in the back of your neck.

The Guitarist

The singer-guitarist also needs to be aware of how bad body use or habits can affect their singing.

A number of guitarists I have worked with experience problems with their breathing and breath control. Holding the guitar awkwardly (from a singer's point of view) causes many of their problems: it can throw their bodies off balance and results in them doing the strangest things to compensate.

People adopt all kinds of unhelpful physical habits and mannerisms when they sing: slumped bodies, stiff shoulders, tense jaws and chins, etc.. The most extreme case I have experienced involved someone who used to jolt his right side up, and then down, by about two inches every time he breathed in. The main problem stemmed from the way he held his guitar. He always played with it slung extraordinarily low on the right and had done so for about ten years. The only possible way he could get enough breath (because his rib cage and lungs were being squashed) was by making an extreme, exaggerated physical movement. By making him aware of this, and by strapping his guitar a bit higher, his singing greatly improved.

Ideally, when you sing, you should stand as I've already described. Many guitarists find their guitars actually help them with their support. If you have your guitar resting against your tummy you can breathe in against it, and use it as an anchor to support your singing through a song.

Guitarists may want to try this version of the diaphragmatic breathing exercise already described:

> *Put your hands on your tummy, just above your tummy button. Breathe in slowly through your nose. Feel your tummy move out. Breathe out in short bursts, on a 'sss' sound, feeling your tummy muscles 'springing' in. You use these muscles to support your voice. Now do the same whilst holding your guitar. Breathe against it. Now play and sing, trying to keep your breath in this low place.*

Guitarist's Chin is a name I've coined for a very common problem amongst guitarists. I have a theory that this strange phenomenon develops as a result of songwriting and playing in the bedroom late at night. Singer-guitarists will often find themselves sitting on the bed strumming away, trying to keep the noise down. Hunched over their guitars, looking for inspiration, they pull their heads back. In a desperate attempt to be as quiet as possible, they either hum or mumble the words with their lips quite closed. Their chins lock and their jaws get very tight, particularly as they sing higher.

In addition, the sound can become very nasal in quality. *Guitarist's Chin*, then, combines several aspects of bad body usage that will inevitably restrict your ability to sing well.

To be quite serious, it is easy to get into bad habits and I know many guitarists for whom this is a real problem. Jaw tension is pretty widespread amongst singers, as I have mentioned before, but *Guitarist's Chin* is a definite contributor! People prone to *Guitarist's Chin* should try the following:

> *Try to keep your lips, not your jaw, forward as you sing in your lower or middle register (as you go higher you will have to open your mouth and the back of your throat more). Practice singing, without playing, with your fingers in 'the groove' (see page 31). This will help to ease any tension and prevent tightening in your jaw. Make sure that you stay open across your chest and shoulders as you play – whether you are sitting or standing.*

You should be at one with your instrument when singing and playing. There are other things you can do to feel freer in your body. For example, learn your guitar parts thoroughly before you accompany yourself. Your playing should be as automatic as possible so that you are freer to think about your singing. If you are playing rhythm guitar, get the rhythm as solid as possible before adding the vocals.

Combining singing and guitar playing well is quite a skill. For pure genius at it, you need look no further than Jimi Hendrix. What you are trying to achieve is a state where you feel that you, your guitar playing and your singing are

KEY POINT

If you play guitar or keyboards as you sing, avoid hunching or 'collapsing' over your instrument and be careful to position your mic in such a way as to keep your body as 'open' as possible.

all one. When you watch footage of Hendrix you just know that was the way he felt. The way he got locked into every aspect of his performance is mesmerizing, totally satisfying and thrilling. He was particularly good at those little guitar fills between vocal lines that help to create an unusually intimate relationship between guitar and voice.

To get on top of playing and singing, either piano or guitar, my advice would be to practice both separately until each one is very secure, before finally putting them together.

Chapter 7
Helpful Practices

The Alexander Technique

It is essential for a you to develop an awareness of how you should be using your body when singing. Something that has helped me to achieve this is the Alexander Technique.

Many people with back problems, or chronic pain sufferers, have found Alexander Technique very helpful.

But you do not have to be experiencing obvious problems to benefit from the technique. In fact it is an assumption amongst Alexander practitioners that most people are 'misusing' their bodies to some extent as a result of learned bad habits – a near-inevitable consequence of modern-day living.

It is difficult to summarize what the technique really is and in fact if you asked a dozen Alexander teachers they would all give you a slightly different answer. For most it represents an entire way of life. Proponents of the technique regard it as an essential guide to how everyone should use their bodies (and minds) healthily in every aspect of their life.

Alexander himself said of the technique:

> 'My technique is based on inhibition. The inhibition of undesirable responses to stimuli, and hence it is primarily a technique for the development of the control of the human reaction.'

The technique is about establishing patterns of good body use, whilst 'inhibiting' or trying to let go of old bad habits (or body misuse). Most people will learn the technique in a 'hands-on' way. The teacher uses their hands to 're-coordinate' the pupil. A lot of work is done with the pupil lying on a table, with the teacher laying their hands on. Sometimes the teacher will work with you sitting in a chair or standing (or moving between the two).

The teacher works gently, focusing on different areas of your body. They may take one arm at a time and then each leg, gently guiding them and encouraging your body to release muscle tensions. They also do a lot of work opening you up across your chest and shoulders. My absolute favorite is having my head 'taken'. You are encouraged to let go of your neck with the teacher taking the full weight of your head in their hands.

As the teacher 're-coordinates' your body, they give you instructions on how to direct your new body use. Much of the emphasis is on 'lengthening and widening' your body and 'freeing' your neck.

It takes a long time to learn the technique and for you to be able to use it in everyday life. Most people don't have the inclination to pursue it fully and it is the 'hands-on' work done by the teacher that they enjoy and get the most benefit from.

I had Alexander lessons for several years and use its main principles in my teaching every day. It has taught me to be 'in tune' with my body as I sing and I have become more aware of myself physically and mentally when I use my voice. I have developed an understanding of what it feels like to sing without excess tension anywhere. It has helped me to sing with an open and relaxed body and a balanced head. Above all, I have learned to be open, wide and free.

There is nothing quite like the feeling you get from having an Alexander lesson. It opens up parts you didn't know existed. In the right hands it makes you feel absolutely brilliant. Having your head 'taken' and your neck lengthened – pure bliss!

A Brief History Of The Alexander Technique

Frederick Matthias Alexander was born in Australia in 1869. In his early twenties he became an actor, specialising in one-man Shakespearean recitals. He soon encountered voice problems. His voice became hoarse and eventually he lost it altogether during a performance. Doctors were unable to help him and prescribed rest. His voice did recover after a few weeks, but as soon as he went on stage again the same thing happened. He therefore deduced that it was what he was doing as he performed that was the root cause of the problem.

He then spent several years examining himself in minute detail in front of mirrors to see what caused his voice loss. He observed, amongst other things, that when reciting he:

Pulled his head back onto his spine;
Put pressure on his larynx;
Gasped air into his mouth.

In time he realised he also did these things during normal speech but it was more exaggerated during performance. Gradually he developed a way of 'inhibiting' these habits and using his body in a more efficient way, enabling him to rebuild his voice completely. He started to teach other people his methods and it became known as the Alexander Technique.

Yoga

Yoga is another practice that has helped me to develop an awareness of how I use my body and also, very importantly, my breath.

Naturally, there are many health benefits to be derived from practicing yoga, but in this book I want to consider specifically how yoga can help your singing.

Yoga is said to describe the 'union of the physical body with the mind and spirit' and therefore the learning of meditation techniques is invariably an important aspect. There are many different types of yoga, of course. I practice Hatha Yoga, which has a real emphasis on breath and getting in touch with your breathing. Hatha Yoga helps you develop an awareness of how to relax and deepen your breath, which is so important when singing.

It is also wonderful for stretching and opening up your body, as well as relieving tension and increasing your energy levels. If you practice yoga, you will develop an awareness of how you are using your body not only when you sing but in everyday life.

I use yoga breathing exercises to help performers to relax fully before they go on stage. The exercises work brilliantly. If you are feeling nervous in any situation – you may have a job interview, or have to give a presentation, for example – the exercises will calm your breath and stop you going into 'panic' breathing. I have described the three-stage breathing earlier. Try it.

It is a very powerful tool.

The meditation side of yoga can also really help you with positive visualization for performance, and I shall be dealing with that later.

General Exercise

Singing involves the whole body and it will therefore help if your general fitness is good. Running and swimming are great – in fact anything aerobic.

In one old, rather quaint, book on choral singing I read, the author recommended 'romping and mushroom-picking' for loosening up the hips. I don't think many of us would be averse to a bit of 'romping', but us city-dwellers are rather starved of opportunities when it comes to mushroom picking.

To be serious, though, be careful when working out in the gym, especially if you are lifting weights or doing sit-ups. Try to avoid putting pressure on your larynx and watch out for any signs of strain. Get a professional coach to help you plan a suitable programme and to check that you are doing the exercises properly. It is not surprising to me that many people develop very 'tight' voices when working out.

SECTION TWO SUMMARY

- How you use the whole of your body has an affect on your singing. In particular, unwanted tensions in certain areas can adversely affect it.

- As you sing, your body should be 'open, wide and free'.

- When you sing, try to maintain a good standing posture: head balanced, shoulders relaxed, chest open, with no tensing of the legs or bottom.

- Do not pull your head back when reaching for high notes, or push down when going for low notes.

- The exercises in this section will help you to become more aware of how you should use your body.

- Singers who accompany themselves on an instrument face particular physical challenges. There are specific things that these people can do to maintain good body use.

- Alexander Technique and yoga are both highly recommended practices for singers.

- Most general exercise, and particularly aerobic exercise, will benefit the singer, although care must be taken in the gym to avoid anything that puts strain on the larynx.

SECTION THREE:
GET SINGING

We have already seen how the raw sound is produced and that what you do with your body can adversely or positively affect it. Now I am going to deal with the real 'ins and outs' of singing – in other words, once you have made the sound, where you send it and what you do with it.

If you take on board the information in this section and put into practice what you learn, you will begin to experience huge improvements in your singing.

Firstly I will talk about *resonance* – how and why you 'resonate' the sound. I will then go on to discuss different *registers* and *voice types* as well as the use of *falsetto* and *vibrato*.

We'll then move on to examine the way you sing words and how this has a huge impact on the sound you make. You will learn about *Singing on the Vowel* – an aspect of technique that has transformed many people's singing overnight.

Then I shall deal with the musical side of things. What is it, in fact, that stands the merely good singers apart from the 'greats'? Included in this section will be a close look at what is meant by *style and phrasing*.

Improvisation is something many singers find difficult and worry about. I am going to suggest a simple approach to get you started. *What key do I sing in?* is a question I am always asked. I shall explain why the question actually doesn't make sense. The subject of *pitch*, *out of tune singing*, *perfect pitch* and *relative pitch* are also all discussed.

Finally, I shall talk about the importance of *warm-up exercises* and give you some to try.

If you have followed the basic instruction up to this point, you should now prepare yourself for some very exciting, accelerated learning.

Chapter 8
Resonance

What Is Resonance?

Resonance refers to the way the bones of the head and upper chest and the air cavities of the pharynx, mouth and nasal passages amplify and change the quality of the basic vocal sound you produce.

In order to appreciate the importance of resonance let's start by considering the following great singers: Frank Sinatra, Billie Holiday, Ella Fitzgerald, Pavarotti, Sting, Aretha Franklin, Freddie Mercury, Elton John and Stevie Wonder. One thing you can say about all of them is that each has an instantly recognizable voice.

So what is it about their voices that gives them their individual quality? Certainly, they all have a strong stylistic identity, being each in their own way masters of style and phrasing (which I shall come on to later). But there is more to it than this. The key to each artist's distinctive 'voice' has its origins in the individual way they produce and *resonate* the sound.

Of course, every singer has a unique voice and this is largely to do with the way we are made. Naturally, there are physical variations between us such as the width of the face, the shape of the cheekbones or jaw, the size of the vocal cords and indeed the various shapes and sizes of the 'resonating' cavities. All these elements combine to give each of us our own individual-sounding voice.

This does not mean, however, that your voice is fixed from birth or that you cannot do anything to change it. On the contrary, you will discover that there are *choices* available to you regarding the type of sound you want to produce, and these are to do with where you decide to 'send' the raw sound once you have made it. As we shall see, you can send the sound into different areas of your body in order to vary its resonance – each area producing a different quality of resonance.

Chest And Head Resonance

In any discussion about resonance probably the most obvious place to start is with the basic distinction between chest resonance and head resonance.

Put simply, when you sing a low note you should feel the vibration in your chest and when you sing higher notes you feel more of the vibrations in your head.

Chest resonance adds warmth to the sound; head resonance adds brightness. Again, you direct the sound through a process of mental control. In a well-balanced voice you can move from one to the other smoothly without any sudden gear changes (see *Registers,* page 61).

Resonance And Vowel Sounds

A good way to demonstrate the differences between chest and head registers is with reference to vowel sounds. As we shall see later (*Singing on the Vowel,* page 80), the singing sound only really happens on vowel sounds and therefore an understanding of how you sing them is absolutely fundamental.

Different vowel sounds have different qualities and resonate in different places. Generally speaking, 'oo' and 'ee' vowels resonate in your head and around the front of your face. These are referred to as 'forward-placed' vowels. 'Ah', 'oh' and 'awe' resonate more in your chest and the back of your throat, and are 'open' sounds. However, by thinking or directing the sound into different places, you can change the basic sound of the vowel, making it darker, lighter or brighter, or more focused.

Furthermore, individual singers prefer certain vowel sounds to others because they find them easier to sing. Different vowel sounds can create tensions in some people: for example, many singers find they tighten their jaws when singing 'ah'; others find they tighten their tongues when singing 'ee'. With practice you can learn to overcome these difficulties.

The following exercise will help you to explore the different qualities of the vowels.

> *Sing part of a song purely on an 'oo' or 'ee' sound instead of singing the words. Now do the same with an 'ah'. You will probably agree that they feel quite different – maybe one is easier than the other. The 'oo' and 'ee' resonate around the front of your face and head. 'Ah' generally resonates further back inside your mouth (and is often harder to control).*
>
> *Sing the 'ee' again. First try it with your mouth in a wide 'grin'; then try it with your lips a bit more closed as if you were to sing an 'oo'. You will probably find the second position easier to control and the sound will be more focused. You should feel the 'buzz' of the singing around the front of your face.*

This forward mouth position also helps you to relax the outer muscles of your larynx and stops you tightening your jaw and tongue. Practice singing songs on an 'oo' or 'ee' with this mouth shape. Many people find it helps their singing to become smoother and more resonant.

Note: As you sing higher, you will need to open your mouth more. If you keep it closed, your singing will tighten up.

Singing on an 'ee' sound doesn't suit everyone, particularly those with bigger or heavier voices. Many singers experience tightness at the base of the tongue; in others it encourages their tongue to arch up and forward. Some people, in addition, will have a great deal of breathiness in the sound.

> *To experience the difference in resonance of the various vowel sounds, now sing the same tune, firstly on an 'oh' sound then an 'ah'. You will feel that the vowels resonate in quite a different place to the 'oo' and 'ee' sounds – more in the back of your mouth and throat. Imagine as you sing that you are directing the sound here, into a wide, open space.*

These vowels are more connected with your chest voice and are darker and more open in quality. You can get a huge amount of power in your voice when you sing with these open vowel sounds.

If you find that you are tightening your jaw on the 'ah' use 'the groove' (see page 31) to help you relax. Be careful as you go higher. You have to allow the sound to move more into your head otherwise it will become stuck in your chest.

Varying Resonance

Moving beyond the basic distinction between head and chest resonance, the key thing to learn about resonance is that you can choose as a singer to 'direct' or 'place' the sound into different areas in order to vary or change its tone.

You can, for example, choose to resonate in a 'chesty', 'nasal', throaty' or 'heady' way. Take these singers: Rod Stewart, Thom Yorke, Neil Young and Tina Turner. You wouldn't have much trouble matching the singer to one of the above distinctive sounds. That is not to say these singers sing exclusively in this way, but that their individual sound features one of these characteristics strongly.

It is what you do with the sound once you have made it that is key. Think of yourself as having access to a kind of 'sound palette'. You can, for example, make the sound darker by sending it into the back of your throat. You can make it brighter by sending it more forward or 'smiling'; and a nasal tone speaks for itself. The choices you make regarding resonance will often be unconscious: your sound is likely to be linked to the sort of music you have listened to a lot or identify with.

There is more to resonance than just a choice of style or tone. Understanding and using resonance represents another piece of the jigsaw. What you do with the raw sound is very important. The sound should not be 'dead' and lifeless; it should 'ring' or, in other words, it should 'resonate'. If you just push it straight out of your mouth, you instantly lose control over it. You need to direct the sound into various different places in your head and body to add volume, warmth, richness, edginess, etc. This is what gives someone's singing its individual character.

As a singer you are your instrument. Guitarists have a sound box, or an amplifier and effects pedals, to produce and resonate their clean or raw sound. Singers don't have that luxury. Obviously, if you sing with a mic, your voice is amplified. You can add some treatments such as reverb, but this won't do much to enrich your tone or give you real sustain. We have seen that if your body is free, the sound you produce will be free. Let's look in more detail at how to do this.

There are various different places you can send the sound, once produced, for different effect: the back of your throat, your chest, the front of your face, your head, or a combination of these.

Simply 'think' the sound into a particular place and – hey presto – it will go there. The power of the mind is so important when singing. I use a great deal of mental imagery when placing the sound.

Thinking Big

When singing, I always think on a large scale. For example, I find it helpful to imagine a singing tube that goes all the way around my body. It starts right at the back of my mouth, opens out into my throat and reaches down into my whole body. I imagine that it is the size of a huge barrel.

As I sing, I feel my whole body filling or resonating with sound. I always have this feeling anchored in my mind and it helps to keep me 'open' in my body.

Similarly, if I am thinking of the back of my throat, my mental image takes on the proportions of an open cavern. If you think 'big' in this way it certainly has a more powerful effect.

Open Throat

One of the chief resonating spaces is the large area at the back of the throat, called the pharynx. As you sing up the scale you should visualize this opening up. You can imagine this as a sort of a yawn in the back of your throat. It is essential to develop an awareness of this space if you are going to have real 'supported' power in your singing.

When you sing using this space you are 'singing with an open throat'. You need to keep this space open as you sing higher to avoid tensing up your larynx.

Some people mistakenly think of the open throat too low down which results in them pressing down with their tongues and, in turn, restricts their singing. Look at the cross-section of the head on page 30. This shows you how big the pharynx is. Imagine the space as if it is a cavern and send the sound here when you are singing. Raise your soft palate (see page 32) – feel it lifting behind your upper back teeth. This will help you get the space open and 'high' enough.

Remember, as you sing higher, the natural tendency is to reach for the notes and raise your larynx. This closes your throat right up. To allow yourself to sing with as much freedom as possible, not only do you need to think of your larynx going down (see *Keeping A Low Larynx*, page 27) but you should combine this with keeping an open space in the back of your throat (remembering to support the sound, of course!). This will give great security and depth to your singing.

The pharynx is not the only place to resonate the sound. If we only sent it there it would become too dark and 'plummy'. I was taught to sing with this 'position' for a number of years. My voice became incredibly strong but lost all its brightness. There is no doubt that working on resonating the sound in this area greatly strengthens your voice but it is all a matter of balance.

Forward Resonance

The area at the front of your face around your sinuses is an important place for resonating. Many opera singers refer to it as the 'mask'. The sinuses themselves don't provide a great amount of resonating space and it is actually the bones in that area that resonate with the frequency.

Resonating in this area is brilliant for adding brightness to the sound. It is what I call 'forward resonance' or 'forward placing'.

> *Rest your hands on your face with your fingers lying across the top of your cheek bones. Pick any mid-range note that feels comfortable and hum on an 'mmm' sound. Think of sending the sound here. You should feel a buzzing sensation. (If you feel it in your chest, try raising the pitch of the note.) Keep practicing as it will come eventually. You are now experiencing forward resonance.*

Don't send the sound into your nose – you don't want it to become too nasal; place it around the sides of your nose and at the top of your cheeks.

Changing And Bending Vowels

As we have seen, you can change the quality of the sound you produce by resonating it in a different place. Sometimes you may want a whole phrase to sound bright, dark or chesty. You can achieve this by 'bending' the vowel sounds so that they resonate in the appropriate place: for a bright and 'ringy' sound, direct it into or around the front of your face and head; for a darker sound, direct it into the back of your throat.

You can also change the vowel quality by 'modifying' it. For example, pure 'oo' and 'ee' sounds primarily resonate in the head. Therefore, if you want to sing these vowels in your chest voice you would:

Change 'oo' to 'u' as in 'foot'
Change 'ee' to 'i' as in 'hit'

This kind of vowel 'modification' really comes into its own when singing higher. As you sing up the scale, regardless of what vowel you are singing, you always need to keep the space in the back of your throat open. You will need to change the shape of the vowels to 'anchor' them here. Let me explain:

If you sing a pure 'oo', 'ee', or 'ah' with any volume on a high note your throat will tighten. To avoid this, open your mouth, keeping the space in the back of your throat open and direct the sound here. The vowels should move towards a 'yawny' 'ah' sound, or '**awe**'. This will help you to support the sound and keep your throat open (remembering to keep a low larynx). You should be aiming for a mixture of openness at the back and bright, forward resonance

The best example I have heard of vowel modification is in Stevie Wonder's *You And I*. Check out the final chorus. As his singing reaches a brilliant climax, he soars up to the word 'I' several times. Listen closely and you will hear him change the words to 'you and **awe**', instead of 'you and **I**'. It is wonderful singing. You can hear the openness in his throat and the huge amount of power he has created. His singing here is almost 'operatic' in quality. (He does add forward, brighter resonance but it is predominantly 'open'.) The way he 'bends' out of the final 'awe' back to 'I' is pure genius!

I have surprised a few singers by pointing out this particular example to them. It is the kind of thing the best singers do naturally and something your ear doesn't easily pick up. It is a demonstration of the way our brain fills in the gaps. Your brain expects a certain word and that's what you hear.

This technique is referred to as 'covering' by classical singers. The sound produced is 'darker' and the larynx position deeper.

Obviously, we can't all be as good as Stevie Wonder, but if you use this approach when singing high notes it can help you immensely.

Mimics And Clones

There are many 'soundalikes' making a living with solo shows or as part of the various 'tribute' bands doing the circuits. Some are clearly better than others. The best mimics copy not only the mannerisms, phrasing and emotional content of the singing they are mimicking, but the resonance and voice quality. They have worked out the exact places where the original artist resonates the sound. It takes patience and a great deal of practice to become very good.

I had the privilege and great pleasure of working with Jane Horrocks on the film *Little Voice*. She is an incredibly talented actor, singer and performer who is hugely committed and totally dedicated to her work. Many people still don't believe she sang all her own songs in that movie, but I can assure you she did – I was there!

Jane hears the particular resonance and quality in a voice and can instinctively copy it. But she doesn't just stop there. For *Little Voice*, we spent many hours dissecting Judy Garland's 'sob', Billie Holiday's fragility and Marilyn Monroe's sensuality. She doesn't arrive at such brilliant performances by accident; she studies the singers in detail, listening to most of their repertoire, reading their biographies and watching them on video. She gets right inside the artist, and that is what makes her renditions so believable.

The scary thing about working with Jane is that you know that she is listening to you all the time and studying your every move and nuance of speech – often to use against you later!

Obviously, many of us are inspired by particular singers and it is often this that gets us interested in singing in the first place.

Unfortunately, many young singers take this too far and become 'clones' – all sounding like their favorite pop singer of the moment. Of course you can learn a huge amount from studying another singer's style and phrasing and get a great deal of pleasure from doing so, but poorer singers may pay attention primarily to the 'style' of a favorite singer at the expense of achieving any real 'substance' to their singing.

The Stage School Sound

Several years ago I was involved in helping to develop a musical in its early stages. We needed to find a girl to play the part of a twelve-year-old. We auditioned fifty girls between the ages of nine and fourteen from a well-known theatre school.

I was dismayed to discover that they all made a very similar sound, with only one actually sounding like a girl and all the rest of them having pushed, 'showy' voices. Indeed, many of them sang very out of tune on the higher notes in an attempt to 'belt' out the notes. They had been taught to sing in a certain way to produce a certain sound that would be appealing in the world of musical theatre.

Apparently no attempt had been made to enhance the individual qualities of their voices. Some people find this type of voice appealing, but it is not for me. Call me old-fashioned, but I think that girls should sound like girls.

I strongly believe in taking people's natural voices and enhancing them with good technique, not 'forcing' them into a mold!

CHAPTER 8 SUMMARY

- Apart from factors relating to the physical differences between people, the key to a singer's individual voice quality lies in the way they produce and resonate the sound.

- A basic distinction is made between chest resonance and head resonance: broadly speaking, when you sing lower notes you will be resonating in your chest; when you sing higher notes you are resonating more in your head.

- You can choose to direct or place the raw sound into different areas in order to create a 'chesty', 'nasal', 'throaty' or 'heady' resonance.

- A chief resonating area is the pharynx. You should always be aware of this space when singing, even when singing with forward resonance.

- The more power you want, the more you will need to focus on resonating in the pharynx.

- It is important to sing with an 'open throat' as you sing higher, to avoid tensing up your larynx.

- Resonating in the area at the front of your face adds brightness to the sound and is known as 'forward resonance'.

- Different vowel sounds have different qualities and resonate in different places.

- By sending the sound into different resonating places you can change the basic sound of a vowel.

- As you sing higher, modify the vowels so that the sound changes to more of an 'awe' sound.

- You can change the resonating qualities of whole phrases by 'bending' the vowel into different resonating places.

Chapter 9
Registers And Voice Types

There is some disagreement amongst singing teachers about registers. Some believe that the voice should function as one and that there is only one register. I believe, however, that there are clear physical differences when singing in the upper and lower parts of your voice, and that the voice should flow freely from one part to another.

There are two main registers, 'head' and 'chest', and it is learning to co-ordinate these and 'smooth' out the changes that is important.

These registers are also referred to as 'head voice' and 'chest voice'. When you are singing in a particular register you will feel the sound vibrate in that area. So, if you are singing in chest voice you will feel the vibrations in your chest and if you are singing in head voice you will feel the vibrations in your head.

Ideally, in a well-balanced voice there will be a smooth transition from one register to another. In order to make it smooth, you need to combine the head and chest registers. This is referred to as the 'middle' voice or register, or even the 'mixed' voice. It is not a true register in itself, but is a combination of the head and chest.

As you go higher, you should sing with more head voice in the sound, gradually letting go of the chest voice. It is vital for the maintenance of a healthy voice that you develop a good middle register. You could view it as a kind of 'crossroads' that ensures that you will move into head voice as you sing higher.

Some singers 'push' the chest register too high. Watch out for this: you could damage your voice if you are not careful.

With a man's voice, most of the time, the sound will be resonating in the chest. A woman, by contrast, will usually be using more head resonance.

What I find interesting is that most people's voices are similar in terms of where the registers actually change. In **men's** voices the change into head voice should start to happen around E flat or E above middle C. This area is referred to as the passage area or *passagio*, and here the singing should be a mixture of chest and head voices (this is the trickiest part for any singer to master). Pure head voice should then be established by about the next F or F sharp.

Women's voices are slightly different. Interestingly, the change from pure chest to head is the same as for men – you should start introducing head voice into the sound around E flat to E above middle C. This is called middle or mixed register. As you sing up the scale you should gradually sing with less chest and more head voice. Be careful around G to A – it is easy to get stuck here. You need to allow the sound to move up into your head. By C or C sharp, an octave above middle C, the resonance should be right in your head. It then stays here, and around F to F sharp it moves again, into a different place in your head.

To help you to get the sound into your head, use some mental imagery. Think of placing the sound in the front of your head. You can picture a long ladder starting at the bottom of your chest and stretching up above the top of your head. With every higher note you sing the resonance wants to be a bit higher and therefore you move a bit further up the ladder.

Caution! This doesn't mean that your larynx is allowed to shoot up as you sing higher. You always need to keep the space in the back of your throat, raise your soft palate and think of your larynx staying low. It is a bit confusing at first because you need to think in several places at the same time. It is a bit like rubbing your tummy and patting your head simultaneously – it gets easier with practice.

A really good example of a contemporary singer who sings with a great mixed register is Amy Lee of the band Evanescence. The brightness of tone it gives her enables her to cut right across the band without straining. I love her voice: she has so much line and power as well as great breath control. I also like the fact that she sings exactly how she wants to and doesn't conform to any stereotypes.

When you sing, it is entirely your choice as to how you use your voice. This information on registers should help you to sing with a well-balanced voice. However, you may choose to take your chest voice high or your head voice low, depending on the sound you want to produce. The most important thing is to understand what you are doing and be able to control it. If you learn to have control of your head voice it will give you many more options when you are singing and will make life easier, as it will prevent the top of your voice from becoming tight and strained.

Pushing The Top

Many rock singers really push their voices as they sing high, getting locked into their chest voices by constantly pushing the top end. In other words, they are singing with too much force too high up. There is no doubt that this can result in damage to your vocal cords. The more pressure you use, the more muscle tension builds up and the more you grip with the muscles around your throat area. This may result in your cords becoming swollen and, if you're not careful, the start of some major vocal problems.

People who sing in this way often find it very hard to develop any head voice, as their cords will not respond in the right way.

Head Voice

To avoid the problems outlined above, you need to know how to get into your head voice without a sudden jolt or change in volume. Incidentally, I am not talking about falsetto here – that's different and we'll come to it later.

Firstly, it is important to use the breath well. It is the single most important factor in achieving even, sustained singing. Keep the breath low in your body and feel free and open. If the breath is working well you are halfway there.

Secondly, never 'reach' for the high notes or pull your head back. Always think 'down' as you go up; think of a see-saw: one end moves up as the other moves down.

In simple terms, when you are singing up the scale you need to allow your voice to move into your head. I find it useful to think of a pathway starting at the front of my face stretching up to the top of my head. As I sing higher, the sound gradually moves up this pathway. With experience you will be able to find this pathway without thinking. The singing will probably feel 'lighter' when you sing in your head voice, but don't regard this as a problem or a weakness. Remember, further up the scale, as you begin to introduce head voice it should be mixed with chest resonance. Gradually let go of the chest voice as you move higher.

It is generally easier for women to find their head voice than men. This is because women's voices resonate naturally more in the head than men's do. Over the years, many singers I have worked with, both men and women, have been reluctant to use any head voice in their singing. They see it almost as an admission of 'failure' not to 'push' their voice to its absolute limits or to virtual breaking point. When they do push their voices, they experience considerable discomfort – sore throats, voice loss, etc.. There is a feeling in the rock and pop world that high singing is only going to sound strong or 'authentic' if the chest voice is pushed to its limits. I strongly disagree.

Sirening is a good way to discover your head voice. Start low in your voice, humming on an 'ng' sound. (Don't place it too far in your nose, it should be behind it, and be careful not to push down with the back of your tongue.) Slide right up and down your voice, as high and low as you like, making a sound resembling a siren. The idea is to get this smooth, with no gear changes. If there are some big 'jolts' don't worry, it will improve with practice.

Many singers with whom I have worked have discovered, with time, the versatility and extra choices that using the head voice gives them, and the different colors and textures that it can incorporate into their singing. (It has provided them with many more options for backing vocals – as an alternative, for example, to singing in falsetto for higher 'BV' parts.) In addition, they have come to regard the use of head voice as good vocal practice which, by way of a bonus, helps them to preserve their voices – especially when gigging.

Let me be very clear, then. If your voice is going to function in a healthy way you must allow yourself to use some head voice in the sound as you sing higher. Without it, you will find it difficult to sustain demanding singing schedules, and your voice will inevitably become strained and damaged.

The Break

Many singers, women particularly, talk about having a 'break' in their voices as they move from one register to another. This usually occurs around G to A above middle C. There should, however, be **no** break and the transition from one register to another should be smooth. As I have said, you achieve this by combining the head and chest voices.

The Belt

'The Belt' is one of my least favorite 'techniques', but is still promoted by some singing teachers. It is predominantly taught to music theatre singers but some pop singers adopt it as well. The technique involves pushing the chest voice as high as possible in order to create that 'music theatre' sound. Apart from anything else, I personally find the belted sound unattractive.

As you can imagine from all I have just said, I regard this technique as fundamentally unhealthy for the voice as it puts far too much strain on it. Indeed, I have met many West End singers with severe voice problems.

There is a belief that the sound will be too 'classical' if you sing with a well-produced voice. It doesn't have to be – your 'ear' will help you make the appropriate adjustments to the sound. If you learn to sing with a well-balanced voice you will be able to sing with a big voice in your upper range without straining. You will have a wider dynamic range and more control.

A friend of mine who has been in many West End shows now sings with what he calls a 'cheating' belt. He 'belted' for many years and suffered from all sorts of voice problems, culminating in nodules. He knew that he couldn't continue in the same way, so he taught himself to support his voice well, employed 'forward placing' and connected this to his chest.

He now has a strong 'mixed' register and head voice. He describes the feeling as singing just behind the bridge of his nose combined with a very open space in the back of his throat. He can sing for hours like this with no pressure on his throat and he produces a really powerful sound. (He also has a very versatile falsetto.) He says that the difference in sound to his 'authentic' belt is hardly noticeable. It is interesting that he calls it a 'cheating belt' as he feels that he is 'cheating' because his singing isn't hurting him!

Voice Types

Singers often ask what their voice type is. These are the main voice types, starting with the highest:

Women

Soprano
Mezzo Soprano
Contralto (alto)

Men

Tenor
Baritone
Bass Baritone
Bass

These names have traditionally been used to describe the range of the human voice. However, it can be very difficult to classify a voice as so much is down to its weight and tone and there are many different classifications within some voice types. This in turn can cause problems if the repertoire given to you is unsuitable and 'pushes' you in the wrong direction. Many mezzo-sopranos, for example, can sing as high as sopranos, but they just don't feel comfortable staying up high for as long.

Ranges

Soprano:
G below middle C up to high C (and beyond). There are different types of soprano depending on the quality of sound and weight of voice: coloratura (high and florid); leggiero (light); lyric (warm tone, long flowing phrase); dramatic (heavy and dark); and spinto (a mixture of lyric and dramatic).

Mezzo-Soprano:
F below middle C to 2nd B above middle C (Voice type is weightier than soprano but lighter than contralto).
These again can be divided into lyric, coloratura and dramatic.

Contralto:
D below middle C to 2nd B flat above middle C. This is the lowest female voice type. Characteristically the voice is weighty with a very warm tone. A true contralto is very rare.

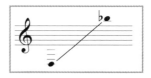

Countertenors:
This is the name for a male voice that is falsetto-dominated. The range extends from F below middle C to the 2nd F above middle C.
Some countertenors vibrate their cords in the same way as normal singers, but the cords are stretched and thinner.

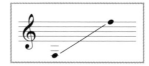

Tenor:
C below middle C to C above middle C.
This is the highest (non-falsetto) male voice type. Tenors, like sopranos, are divided into different types: lyric, spinto, dramatic, and *Heldentenor* (heroic).

Baritone:
2nd G below middle C to high G sharp.
Weightier and richer than a tenor voice. There is classification within baritones also: light, lyric, dramatic, Verdi.

Bass Baritone:
Low F to high F sharp.
The voice quality is lighter than a bass.

Bass:
2nd F below middle C to F above middle C.
The lowest male voice type.

Basso profundo is the name given to a very deep bass whose range is 2nd C below middle C to E above middle C.

Many of us know where we feel happiest singing, whether it's high, low or mid-range and don't really need to know whether we are soprano or tenor, etc. Obviously if you sing in a choir or sing classical music you will need to know. Also if you sing musical theatre repertoire it is helpful to know your voice type.

Repertoire is often published in several editions – in different keys for high or low voice, for example. For some people it is quite obvious what voice type they are. Those in the middle should take care. If, for example, having always thought of yourself as a soprano, you then join a choir and find you are straining, don't be afraid to admit it and ask to change to the alto part.

Tessitura is a term used to describe the range of the voice or a piece of music. If a song is said to have a high tessitura, this would mean that most of the notes of the song would lie quite high.

As I have already said, just because you can reach certain notes it doesn't mean you will necessarily be comfortable singing in this part of your voice all the time. If the tessitura of the material is consistently high or low it may be too much for you.

CHAPTER 9 SUMMARY

- There are two main registers: head and chest. It is important to co-ordinate the two and smooth out the movement from one to the other.

- To make this transition smooth, the head and chest registers combine. This is referred to as the 'middle' or 'mixed' voice or register.

- Although there are clear differences between male and female voices, they are remarkably similar in terms of where the registers actually change.

- 'Pushing the top' or singing too high in chest voice as an alternative to moving into head voice is a common cause of voice strain amongst singers.

- It is very important, therefore, to know how to get into your head voice without a sudden jolt or change in volume.

- To allow your voice to move into your head as you sing up the scale, it is useful to think of a pathway that starts at the front of your face and stretches up to the top of your head, along which the sound climbs or moves.

Chapter 10
Falsetto

If you are not sure what falsetto sounds like, think of the Bee Gees or Justin Timberlake. Falsetto refers to the highest part of a man's voice – the bit they had before their voices broke, or the 'choirboy' part. It is used a lot in pop and R&B singing to add a lightness to the tone as well as a touch of flamboyance – as some people associate 'high' with 'good'.

Having a good falsetto definitely gives you more options at the top of your voice and more choices of texture. It can also help to preserve your voice as you can use it as an alternative to 'pushing' the top.

I like the sound of a well-produced falsetto – one that is focused and that the singer moves into smoothly. Achieving this can be technically tricky, but mastered with practice.

I don't agree with them, but some people dislike the use of falsetto and think of it as a complete 'cop-out', preferring the top of the voice to be 'pushed' and 'chested'.

The term 'falsetto' actually means 'false' voice. This would seem to suggest that it is not a legitimate 'voice', but that is simply not the case. Falsetto is a definite, physically identifiable voice in its own right. Experiments show that when singing in falsetto your vocal cords are lengthened, tense and thinned and there is minimal vibration. The airflow creates a hole so that the cords don't come together fully.

From as early as the thirteenth or fourteenth century, it appears likely that male singers sang using falsetto. Certainly, throughout the history of Western music, men have tried to extend their range by blending head voice with falsetto. Classical male singers who sing mainly using falsetto are referred to as *countertenors*.

Castrato is the name given to a male singer who was castrated before reaching puberty. This practice was performed mainly in Italy from the sixteenth Century to the early 1900s. It was an attempt to keep the purity of tone and high voice of the prepubescent singer, but it didn't always work! Only one castrato, Alessandro Moreschi, has ever been recorded and the sound is quite extraordinary.

The alternative to castration for men who want to sing high is to develop their head voice and falsetto – quite a motivation, I would have thought!

There is some disagreement over the terminology. Some teachers believe that the head voice should be called falsetto. However, as I have tried to show, there is an obvious difference between the two.

When you sing in falsetto you will feel that the sound occurs in a similar place to the head voice, but the tone and resonance produced are very different. Your falsetto may feel a bit 'disembodied' but this does not mean that it has to be fragile and weak.

The falsetto of many rock and pop singers is very strong and cuts right across a band. Listen to Freddie Mercury or, for a more contemporary example, the flamboyant Justin Hawkins of The Darkness. Furthermore, to develop and strengthen your falsetto, apply the same principles of good technique (maintaining an open throat, supporting, etc.) that you would use in the rest of your voice.

Working with Falsetto

Men with naturally high voices tend to sing in head voice in the upper range, only moving to falsetto when it gets very high. Men with lower voices, who have a more limited head voice, start their falsetto lower. It is knowing just where to change that causes confusion for many singers.

Remember, it is vital if you wish to have a well-balanced voice, that you develop a strong and secure head voice. You shouldn't bypass this and only sing in falsetto at the top.

You should be singing with some head voice around E/ E flat above middle C. For those of you with lower voices, you might not be able to take this any higher than F/F sharp. Don't worry if you can't, it is simply the limit of your range. If you want to sing higher then go into falsetto.

Women also have a falsetto, but very few use it. Again, many women incorrectly refer to their head voice as falsetto. In fact, it is that peculiarly high place in which Mariah Carey, for example, does her 'squeaks'. The notes up here, above normal head voice, are sometimes called 'super-high' notes, or the 'whistle' register.

A strong falsetto can be a very useful tool. It can help you to extend melodies and vary textures. It is also extremely useful when singing backing vocals, particularly high, blended harmonies. Used as an alternative to high, 'shouted' choruses when gigging, it has the added advantage of helping you to protect your voice from undue strain.

It is fair to say that many singers do not use falsetto as well as they could. It is the change from full voice into falsetto and back that causes many singers problems. Often there will be a 'jolt' as the sound gets suddenly weaker or louder. You will frequently hear male singers attempting, but not really making, the change from chest to falsetto.

It is hard to blend falsetto with the rest of your voice, and it can sound disconnected from your normal voice – resulting in a sudden loss of resonance and character. With practice you can make these changes more even.

Always keep the breath low in your body (around your lower abdomen). Don't tense your shoulders or snatch the breath into your chest. Keep your body relaxed. It is vital for the sound to be properly supported. Let the sound 'ring' around your head as if it is in a big bell tower.

> *Sing the first five notes of a scale up and down on a 'mee' sound in falsetto (starting around an E above middle C). Repeat the pattern, raising it each time by a semitone (a half step). Then sing it on 'oo' and then 'ah'. Which is the trickiest? – probably 'ah' (it is a more 'open' sound).*

Experiment by placing the sound forward as you go higher. Then sing it with a 'yawny' open throat. Play around with it and see what works for you.

Many singers find if they place the falsetto very forward, almost around the top of the nose and around their sinuses, it helps to free up the sound and make it more focused. Others prefer feeling it right up in their head with a very open throat to give them power.

It will probably be easier for you to go from chest voice to falsetto at first (rather than head voice to falsetto). Practice the change from low to high and then try it the other way round – going from high to low. Keep working the links and it will become more reliable. Think 'down' when you are moving in or out of falsetto – it will help to keep your larynx stable.

If you strain your voice, often the first part to 'go' is your falsetto. If those poor vocal cords become swollen through 'pushing' and misuse they just cannot stretch and be free enough for the falsetto to happen.

A few years ago an artist with whom I had been working had been a naughty boy and thrashed his voice while singing at a couple of large arena gigs. I was called in to try and help out as his falsetto had totally disappeared.

Fortunately, with careful warming up (an issue that will be discussed later in do's and don'ts) he more or less got it back– although he couldn't sing anything on an 'ah' sound (it is an open sound and you use more air to produce it than you do with 'oo' and 'ee'). So he had to cheat and change all his vowel sounds to 'ee's and 'oo's when singing in falsetto. He survived the gig and I am pleased to say had a couple of days' rest and was fine.

Some people will never like falsetto singing but I think it is a useful weapon to add to your armory. Besides, where would we be without, for example, The Beach Boys' 'Good Vibrations'? There are some artists, like the Bee Gees who sing in it almost exclusively. However you choose to use falsetto, make sure you are doing so because you really want to, and not purely as a substitute for singing in head voice where your technique is lacking.

Choristers And Children's Voices

I defy anyone not to be moved by the pure voice of a good choirboy: there is such innocence and clarity in the sound. Surprisingly, however, the majority of choristers fail to develop into equally good adult singers. Indeed, I have seen it stated that only 2% of choristers ever turn into fine adult singers, and I suspect the problem is due to voice misuse at around the time their voices break.

Some of it can be blamed on shouting in the playground and at football games, and of course, at their parents. But, more worryingly, many boys are forced to sing too high for too long. From the ages of about 12 to 15 their voices undergo major physical changes. Sensible vocal practice would be to let them gradually sing lower parts and not put their voices under any strain.

This is true of all children, whatever type of music they are performing. Many experts will not allow serious voice training to start until the age of 17 in girls and 18 to 19 in boys. You need to use common sense here. Of course it is all right to continue singing, and, in fact, I teach many teenage girls and boys. It is good to begin to get to grips with breath control and tone production, but you just have to take it easy and not push their voices if you want them to last a lifetime.

The Breaking Voice

Many boys have a traumatic time when their voices break. It used to be advised that they stop singing during this period, but modern thinking (with which I agree) is that it is generally fine as long as care is taken. Some boys hardly notice their break happening as it does so gradually. Other boys, however, experience something more sudden. Some voices take a lot longer than others to settle down. Many boys become distressed at losing their higher range or 'bright' tone.

I try to help them to be patient and enjoy the different qualities of their 'new' voices. I never allow them to force their voices. I believe that it is good for boys to sing during this time. If you leave it, their voices can become very breathy and they may find it hard to 'start up' again. Besides, for those who love singing, getting them to give it up for any substantial length of time would be like asking them to go without computer games, fries, or TV.

CHAPTER 10 SUMMARY

- Falsetto refers to the highest part of a man's voice – not a 'false' voice, but another, physically different, voice in its own right.

- A strong falsetto should not be regarded as a 'cop-out' but as a very useful tool to have at your disposal.

- However, in order to have a well-balanced voice it is vital that you develop a secure head voice and do not bypass this in favor of a leap straight into falsetto.

- Many singers find the easiest place to sing in falsetto is forward, almost around the top of their nose and sinuses.

- Care should be taken with boys whose voices are breaking.

Chapter 11
Vibrato

Technically, vibrato is an oscillation in the pitch of the singing sound. It adds color and warmth, but varies widely in nature and use. It occurs naturally, but, as we shall see, an experienced singer will use vibrato the way an artist applies color to their canvas. Artistic decisions are made about which colors to use and where.

As I have said before, the best singers have distinctive voices. Whether or not you happen to like a particular voice, you can usually identify a well-known singer on first listening. Many things combine to make up a singer's individual tone or 'sound'. As we have seen, how and where a singer resonates the sound is one important element: they may favor a breathy, nasal, chesty or heady sound. Phrasing and accent are also distinguishing features, but use of vibrato is another major component.

Classical purists believe there is only one correct way of producing vibrato – the sound an opera singer would make, as it is a free and supported sound. In opera singing, vibrato is used throughout. For most opera singers, the idea of turning vibrato 'on' and 'off' as a textural technique represents something artificial or 'manufactured'.

I had a singing teacher once who was a brilliant technician and a real purist. He was absolutely appalled when he discovered that I sang other styles of music. He believes there is only one 'correct' way to produce the voice. I disagree. It is up to you as a singer how you use your voice and how you produce the sound – and, for that matter, what kind of music you sing! I really don't believe any one singing genre is better or 'more important' than another. What concerns me is singing well, with a good technique, regardless of singing style.

Some singers of early classical music choose to sing with no or very little vibrato, and many musicians debate endlessly as to whether this is how it was originally done. However, there is no doubt in my mind that some singers sound lovely without a heavy use of vibrato.

Rock and pop singers generally do not use masses of vibrato in their singing. Some do, but the sound is usually a lot drier than that of the classical singer. Rock and pop delivery or style is more 'conversational' and direct. There are, in effect, many different ways of using vibrato, and its use varies according to the particular genre of singing in question.

Most pop singers use vibrato sparingly. Soul and R&B singers use it more evenly. If you listen to a Stevie Wonder song you will probably be surprised by how much he mixes and matches – often using no vibrato, or just bringing it in at the last moment. He has a natural, 'smiley' vibrato and uses it very tastefully.

Show singers utilize a deliberate, exaggerated, often nasal vibrato. One of the most extreme is Ethel Merman, famous for, amongst others, her over-the-top rendition of 'There's No Business Like Show Business'. A pronounced yet silky vibrato is very much part of the style of the great crooners, such as Nat King Cole, Bing Crosby or Sinatra.

Even within rock and pop, its use varies widely. Singers such as Sheryl Crow and Alanis Morissette don't use any vibrato to speak of. Their style is very direct – they literally 'push' the words out. The vibrato of, say, Elvis Costello or David Bowie is particularly deliberate and distinctive. Bonnie Raitt uses vibrato very evenly and will alter its speed, depending on the tempo of the song: in slow ballads it is gentle and lazy (a slow oscillation). Compare this to the incredibly fast vibrato of the Bee Gees. Many singers such as Sting use it just at the end of a phrase, or on sustained notes.

Guitarists And Vibrato

Interestingly, several guitarists I know have studied vibrato very closely. They have listened to their favorite players and tracks, working out the exact speed and quality of vibrato that they particularly like. They will tell you about the difference between B.B. King's very fast, intense vibrato and the much slower vibrato typically employed by someone like Albert Collins.

The interesting thing about the use of vibrato and note-bending in blues playing is that the original great blues guitarists were in fact trying to make their instruments resemble the human voice. The blues and blues-orientated music are all about communicating what you are feeling to your audience. The choice of vibrato in the hands of the great guitar players like those mentioned above closely reflects the emotion being put across. An emotionally intense passage, perhaps expressing anger or frustration, would require a quicker, more intense vibrato; a more subtle passage dealing with feelings of love or sadness would call for a more subtle, slower vibrato. Good singers also vary their vibrato in this way according to the emotional requirements of the song they are singing.

Eric Clapton once said that one of the most difficult things for any guitar player to accomplish is to produce their own natural-sounding vibrato, the point being that it takes time for the vibrato to become 'natural', for its use to become, in a sense, automatic. The best guitarists and the best singers ultimately reach a stage where they don't have to think about when or how to add it because it becomes a question of 'feel'. Furthermore, many have created a vibrato in their playing or singing that is recognizably their own.

Incidentally, in a discussion about how guitarists imitate the sound of the voice, it is worth mentioning that this can be a two-way process. Listen to the singing of Anthony Kiedis from the Red Hot Chili Peppers (who, incidentally, uses vibrato very sparingly) and notice how his singing often echoes the string bending and other licks favored by guitarists.

Working On Your Vibrato

If you have a well-supported voice, you will produce vibrato naturally. I would say, the freer the voice, the freer the vibrato. Furthermore, you can use it in any way you choose. You can make it long, or short; you can use it throughout a phrase or just at the end. In other words, control over vibrato gives you many more choices in your singing.

Many singers want to improve their vibrato, making it more consistent, even and controlled. However, vibrato is a bit of a mystery for some singers.

If you have no vibrato at all, I suspect your voice is too tight. You will probably be 'clamping' with the outer muscles of your larynx. A constant theme of mine is that your singing should be free and not 'held' anywhere. Always remember to breathe low and stay relaxed. You should continually check for any unwanted tension anywhere in your body, but especially in the throat, jaw and tongue areas. As I said before, if you are doing all the major things right, your vibrato should occur naturally. In this sense it is a good check on your technique.

Some singers produce an artificial, forced-sounding vibrato. It can sound all right but never free and relaxed.

Vibrato Exercises

The following exercises are designed to help you understand a bit more about vibrato, how you make it happen, and how you can control it.

This exercise is in three parts:

> *1.   Hold a single mid-range note. Try to use vibrato for the whole length of the note. Relax your body, jaw and tongue. Take a slow, deep breath. Think of drawing the sound in, not pushing it out, keeping it supported. Let it travel into the back of your throat.*

Start off on the vowels 'ooh', 'ee', and 'ah'. Stay relaxed – massage your jaw and chin with your hands as you are singing.

> *2.   Hold a single note, but this time try bringing in the vibrato halfway through the note. Still draw the sound in.*
>
> *3.   Repeat as above; just bring the vibrato in at the very end of the note.*

Try making the vibrato by sending the sound into the front of your mouth, keeping your lips forward. 'Think' about the sound you want to make. Try speeding it up and slowing it down. Try singing the whole note with vibrato or using it just at the end. Experiment. The confusing part is remembering to draw the sound into your body at the same time.

You have to be supporting strongly to be able to use vibrato properly.

Now, try varying the sound, sending it more into your nose and then into the back of your throat (this will sound a bit heavier and more 'operatic' – particularly if you are supporting well). Play around with it. If you find a sound you like, work with it. Don't worry if the vibrato is not happening initially – it will eventually.

When you have practiced on the vowels, move on to words. Start with single words, progressing to a few lines from a song. Try using vibrato throughout and then just at the end of a phrase or on the more sustained notes. It is up to you to choose how you use it.

Many singers find it feels a lot easier to sing using a mic with plenty of reverb applied. However, you should be able to add your own vibrato. I have known professional singers who rely far too heavily on using a mic, and in fact have no natural vibrato at all. This is very limiting because in a dry acoustic it will become almost impossible to sing, as your voice will become very tight. So start working on your vibrato and have yet another string to your bow.

CHAPTER 11 SUMMARY

- Vibrato is the vibrating of the singing sound and should arise naturally from a well-supported voice.

- Good singers will vary their vibrato according to the emotional requirements of a song.

- If you have no vibrato at all, you probably have too much tension or tightness around your larynx.

- Exercises given in this section will help you to produce vibrato and learn how to control it.

Chapter 12
Singing On The Vowel

When you sing, what is it exactly you sing? Songs? Words? Notes? How about vowels? Sounds dumb? Trust me. If you take on board what I have to say about 'singing on the vowel' you could be on the verge of a massive breakthrough. For many singers, learning about 'singing on the vowel' is a pivotal moment in their lives. Whatever style of music you are singing, learning about the importance of singing vowels will make a huge difference to you.

I have talked a lot about resonance and the different qualities that the vowels have. I mentioned the specific differences between, say, the brighter, more 'forward' EE vowel and the darker AH vowel. In fact, creating vowel sounds is absolutely fundamental to your singing.

You need to concentrate on the vowel in order to gain control of your singing, and enable you to sustain a musical line or, in other words, sing in a *legato* way. Let me explain further.

Try singing and holding a note on a selection of consonants: D, T, G, F, K, for example – it's impossible, right? True, you can make a humming sound on an 'm' and 'n', but that's about it. The actual singing sound only happens on the vowel sounds, which, in the above exercise, you can't help sliding into. Therefore, it follows that if you want your singing to flow, you must spend as much time as possible singing the vowels and making the most of each vowel's resonance. This is, of course, why singing exercises are sung on the vowel sounds (see pages 110-120).

The main vowel sounds we use when singing are the following:
'**ah**' as in heart, '**awe**' (yawn), '**oh**' (got), '**o**' (low), '**oo**' (moo), '**i**' (lid), '**ee**' (tree),'**uh**' (shut), and '**e**' (met). In any song, any note should only really be held on one of these sounds.

Let's see how it works.

Take for instance the word 'love'. Sing it on any note and hold it for as long as you can. Think about the sound you make; its mainly an 'uh' sound (or 'er' if you're singing with an American accent). Try it again. This time hold the 'uh' sound and count (in your head!) to 4, then bring in the 'v'. Do it crisply; don't slide into it. Look in a mirror and try it. Are you trying to close your lips before you actually get to the 'v'? Try not to anticipate the consonant – it stops you making the most of your resonance. If the consonant comes in too early it cuts the sound dead – there is just no way you can hold the note.

Okay, one word is not too bad, but let's move on to putting words together into a phrase or line. If you want to be able to sing a legato line you must be able to sing through every vowel. Firstly, say these words: "Will you still love me".

The sound pretty much stops between the words and is quite detached. Now try linking the consonant from the end of one word to the beginning of the next. This will keep the sound flowing right the way through. It should go something like this:

Wi – llyou – sti – luh – vme

Now sing it. Try it your usual way first and then my way. Hold onto each vowel and sing right through them. Feel the sound resonating. Try it first on just one single note and then vary the pitches. You should begin to notice the difference. The more you apply this approach to your singing, the easier it gets, and the more sense it makes.

Once you are singing the vowels, remember to let them cruise on the platform of supported air.

You will find some words trickier than others. Watch out for those ending in 'y'. They can make a double vowel sound (diphthong). Take 'cry'. This is made up by joining 'ah' and 'ee' together: cr-ah-ee.

KEY POINT

You can only really hold notes on vowel sounds which is why, for example, singing exercises are sung mainly on the vowels 'ah', 'awe', 'oh' and 'ee'.

Try staying on the 'ah' for as long as possible before bringing in the 'ee'. This will give you a rounder sound. If you move to the 'ee' too quickly the sound will be thinner. Sometimes you may want that effect, but it is good to be able to have the choice.

Of course, this is a general guide. The aim is to help you sustain a smooth (legato) line. This is naturally desirable in slower numbers, but, interestingly, you have to work even harder at it in faster ones since the words come more quickly.

All this does not of course mean that consonants are unimportant. On the contrary. They are equally important but for different reasons. Without strong consonants, the lyrics would lose their meaning and the song would lack energy.

Not only do you need consonants to make the words clear (what we refer to as 'good diction'), but they can also be used percussively. They are an essential part of what gives singing its groove and rhythm. It is the ability to 'spring off' consonants onto vowels that you need to work on. This will not only add more groove but ultimately much more line to your singing.

Learning to sing on the vowel is one of the most effective tools you can have to improve and enhance your singing. It will make the difference between your singing sounding like (for all you guitarists out there) a soaring Satriani solo or a string of sausages.

Of course, a singer has to pay attention to the meaning of words in order to interpret and put across a song powerfully. But listen to the vowel element in the songs of any of the best and most convincing singers you know, and you will see how important it is.

When I first came across this method of singing the words, I wrote out all the songs that I was learning in a similar way to my example above. After about three weeks it had become second nature. Try approaching songs in this way; it is well worth the effort.

Breathing Within A Song

I have already emphasized how crucial control of the breath is to singing. I want to reinforce something very important. When you sing, the breath should flow in a controlled yet relaxed way. Breathing in a relaxed way is the most important point of technique to master. If you get this right, pretty much everything else will follow.

If you have been practicing your breathing exercises you should already be feeling the benefits. Hopefully you now have a much greater awareness of your breath and are developing more control over it.

When it comes to singing a song, however, things start to get a bit more difficult. You may find you begin the song with plenty of air, but by the time you've finished the first verse or reached the chorus, the breath has become tight and, before you know it, your old habits have reared their ugly heads.

Your focus should be on your out-breath. The out-breath is the relaxing part of your breathing cycle.

As soon as you get to the end of a phrase, breathe in. Don't hang around in a state of limbo waiting to gasp in the air like a goldfish just before you sing. If you do snatch in the air, you will tighten across your chest and shoulders and your breath will be too shallow. Your body will become tense and the sound breathy, and you will only be able to sing short phrases. In addition, you will probably get head rushes.

Breathing in as soon as you have used up the air makes you take in the air in the right way. Try it. Hands on tummy; sing a phrase. As you finish, your tummy should be 'in'. You should be able to feel some muscle tension here. If you support the ends of phrases properly, this will happen naturally. Breathe in (your tummy should come out), then, when you're ready, start the next phrase. If there is not much time to breathe, then shorten the first phrase to give yourself more time. Never snatch in the breath. Keep this cycle going through a whole song. Don't be tempted to top up the breath in between or sneak in a little extra one.

Obviously, if there are significant spaces between phrases, this will not apply. But remember always to breathe at least one whole beat before coming in.

If you master this way of managing your breath, it will have a huge impact on your singing. You will be able to sing longer phrases, have much more control overall, and your breathing and therefore your body will be relaxed.

If your breathing does become tight, breathe out hard a few times through your nose or mouth.

You will notice that as you gain more control over your breathing, you have to start to sing in a different way. If you are used to singing only short phrases and gasping in the air, it is hard to break this habit. You need consciously to make yourself sing longer phrases, otherwise, however good your general breath control has become, you will still continue to take in too much air through constant 'topping up'.

You will need to challenge yourself – habits are very hard to break. This does not mean you have to alter your phrasing: just avoid breathing in all the gaps. Only take in air when you need to – use up your air first.

This can be a tricky thing to get your head round initially. It is hard to believe that by breathing less frequently you will have more air, but it really is true. You will be amazed at how much more control you will have.

A good way to practice singing long phrases is mentally to rehearse singing them (i.e. without any sound). Put your hands on your tummy. Breathe in. Now imagine you are singing the phrase. Let the air out as if you were singing, but don't make any sound. If your breath can last for the whole phrase, you are ready to sing it properly. I find it helps to focus on the breath if I keep my eyes closed, as I can internalize my thoughts more easily.

CHAPTER 12 SUMMARY

- Learning to 'sing on the vowel' is a pivotal moment in the lives of most singers.

- When you sing, you can only really hold notes on vowel sounds.

- The main vowel sounds used in singing are: **'ah'** as in heart, **'awe'** (yawn), **'oh'** (got), **'o'** (low), **'oo'** (moo), **'i'** (lid), **'ee'** (tree), **'uh'** (shut), and **'e'** (met).

- In order to sing in a legato (smooth or 'joined-up') way you need to be able to sing through every vowel.

- Consonants are important in their own right: for making the words clear, and for percussive effect.

- In order to achieve 'groove' and line in your singing you need to learn how to 'spring off' consonants onto vowels.

- You should focus on the out-breath when you sing a song.

- You should aim to breathe in as soon as you have used up the air – never 'snatch' in the breath.

- If there is not much time to breathe between phrases then shorten the first phrase to give yourself more time.

- Keep a natural cycle of breath going and don't be tempted to top up the breath within phrases or steal extra ones.

Chapter 13
Style And Phrasing

We have talked a lot about how you make the sound and how to vary and improve its quality. Now it is time to tackle singing songs. I want you to understand what makes certain singers special. Yes, it is partly down to the sound of their voice and the material they sing, but the roots of their success lie in what they do with the sound once they have made it. It is not only how they sing the words that is important, but where they put them. Is the singer, for example, behind the beat, on it, or in front of it? Let me explain.

Feel

The songs that stay with us are those that move us in some way – they have energy, emotion or both. Delivering a song is not just about singing a correct melody and lyric in a technically perfect way. It is also about interpretation, style and what we call 'feel'. The singing has to be convincing: we need to feel that the singer is emotionally involved or 'believes' in the song for us to get involved as a listener.

A singer's impact depends on their interpretation of a song. If the song were sung as it is written in a songbook, it would sound 'straight' and lifeless. There are many different elements involved in putting across a song well. A singer, in order to add meaning or color, may pick out certain words for emphasis by varying their rhythm, lengthening or shortening them, giving them more weight, or embellishing or almost 'speaking' them. But when we talk about interpretation we are not solely concerned with what we do with the words or with raw emotion.

When you listen to a good singer you are aware that everything sounds just right. The best singers appear to be able to put a song across with ease. This does not happen by accident. Like any instrumentalist, these singers will have listened to hundreds of other singers over the years. Many will have borrowed licks or phrasing from their own favorites, tried out lots of ideas and, gradually, have become confident enough to develop their own individual style or feel.

Singing On/Off The Beat

Singers, not being machines, never really sing perfectly on the beat. These small imperfections of timing, whether ahead or behind the beat, lie at the root of what we call 'feel'. Singers can make a song more exciting and interesting by varying the rhythmical phrasing – by starting words or phrases earlier ('pushing') or later ('sitting behind the beat').

While vocal melodies are frequently sung 'across the beat', it can at times be very effective pointedly to sing some lines bang on the beat for percussive impact. An interesting exercise is to listen to a track with a metronome click. You will be able to hear exactly where the stresses are coming. It is the rhythm of the singing that gives it its groove.

Developing good feel relies on extending your musical vocabulary. Start by listening closely to your favorite singers. Notice where they vary a repeated melody– say, in a second verse or a final chorus – maybe simply by taking it higher. If the line is repeated in an identical way, the impact isn't the same.

> **KEY POINT**
>
> *Good singers will vary the rhythmical phrasing of a song by singing before, behind or dead on the beat. This lies at the root of what we call 'feel'.*

Also listen for changes to the rhythm of a phrase: some words may be stretched or shortened. As we have seen, you need to be aware when a singer is singing across the beat or when they are right on it. The singer has to consider the rhythm not only of the music but also of the words. The best singers really listen and react to the instruments and are rhythmically locked into the track.

At this point, it is worth mentioning the importance of timing your breath correctly. If the breath is late, then your entry will be late. You should aim to take a breath approximately one beat before entry (this will prevent you from 'snatching' in the breath). You need to make space to breathe. You have to breathe in the right place in order not to 'throw' a phrase. You will need to come off a line or phrase early to give yourself time to breathe in the faster sections of a song. (But see *Breathing For Singing*, page 20).

Incidentally, the ends of words and phrases should always be rhythmic and never sloppy. If you end phrases crisply, this maintains the energy of the song. Even in slow ballads the placing of the consonants adds to the overall feel of the song.

Dynamics

Dynamics are the variations in volume – the 'louds' and 'softs' – a singer chooses to use for effect. They are the key to the 'build' of a song – if you like, to its emotional shape. Good singers use dynamics effectively.

The simplest dynamic pattern would be a song that starts off softly and then builds to a loud climax. A more subtle shape might take the form of a quiet start, followed by a dynamic build, followed by a small drop, and ending with a big 'up'. You don't, however, always have to sing a high note loudly or end a song full 'belt' – the opposite can be very effective. Consider Bryan Adams' '(Everything I Do) I Do It For You'. The song has a great build and the choruses are big. However, he brings the singing right down to end sensitively and with intensity.

> **KEY POINT**
>
> *Singers use dynamics – 'louds' and 'softs' – to help create the emotional shape of a song.*

Singers of classical music or other score-written music will, of course, be familiar with dynamic instructions such as *forte* (loud), *piano* (soft), *crescendo* (get louder), *diminuendo* (get softer) etc, but to what degree the individual singer responds to these suggestions is still to a certain extent up to interpretation. Some singers are innately musical and will interpret the same piece of music far more powerfully than others.

In popular music it is through improvising or ad-libbing that a singer makes a song his or her own. Improvisation can range from changing a word or line, to changing whole phrases and introducing new ones. For your improvisation to sound convincing you have to be confident and bold (see *Improvisation,* page 90).

CHAPTER 13 SUMMARY

- In addition to singing a song well technically, delivering a song has a lot to do with interpretation, style and 'feel'.

- Small imperfections of timing, whether ahead of or behind the beat, lie at the root of what we call 'feel'.

- Good singers vary the rhythmical phrasing of a song for emotional effect.

- The singer has to consider the rhythm not only of the music but also of the words.

- Dynamics are the 'louds' and 'softs' a singer chooses to use for effect. Their use helps to create the emotional shape of a song.

Chapter 14
Improvisation

The term improvisation as it is used here refers to the way an individual singer chooses to embellish or make excursions from the original melody of a song. It is the means by which they interpret a song in their own, individual way.

Billie Holiday was arguably one of the most influential singers of the last century. It is said of her that she never sang any song the same way twice. Her interpretation was second to none. She had the ability to make a song her own by altering its melody and phrasing, and thereby its emotional complexity and impact.

Many of you reading this may not have aspirations to be great jazz singers, but it is the development of jazz and blues singing that lies at the heart of improvisation in many forms of music. It is fair to say that improvisation came naturally to the likes of Billie Holiday, and it is precisely this that worries some people. While they may view themselves as quite decent singers, they don't necessarily see themselves as natural improvisers.

Even Billie Holiday, however, listened to a lot of music and learned about improvisation through experience and experimentation. In this section I am going to suggest some practical things you can try to get you started – there are indeed elements of improvisation that you can learn and begin to build into your singing.

You sometimes hear songs sung – regardless of musical style – the same way throughout, without any variations of phrasing or melody. It can be pretty dull. It is always more interesting and exciting if the singer 'lets go' a bit, and maybe takes the chorus higher or puts in some ad libs.

The majority of rock and pop songs follow a similar format. Commonly, a first verse will be sung 'straight', the second with a little embellishment, and the final verse taken higher. Sometimes this final verse will be taken quite a long way from the original melody. The choruses gradually build in a similar way.

There are various different ways you can improvise. Don't be frightened. Improvising doesn't have to mean amazing George Benson-type scatting or Beyoncé-style 'licks'. At the heart of improvisation is the ability to take a song and alter the phrasing and/or melody to make it your own. This applies to jazz as well as rock and pop music.

The first step towards improvising is to listen closely to a lot of good singers. Tap out the beat of a song. Work out whether the singer is singing behind the beat, on the beat, or ahead of it. It is surprising what you can hear when you really listen.

Now listen to the melody. Does the singer vary it at all and, if so, in what way? Do they alter just the odd word or whole phrases? Do they take sections higher or lower?

Once you have begun to work out what other singers do, you can start to have a go yourself.

> *Sing the first line of a song. Experiment by changing the rhythm of the words slightly. Try delaying the word on the second beat, for example; then try it dead on the beat, and then slightly before the beat. Now have a go on other words. Keep the variations that you like. It is important to be able to 'pull' the words around. You need to feel you have control of the song, and that you don't have to sing every phrase exactly as 'written'.*
>
> *Now try a verse and chorus using this same approach, sometimes laying back behind the beat, and sometimes 'pushing' the singing on. Mix it up: sing some lines slowly; speed through others a little more quickly; vary the pace. Sometimes the meaning of the words will suggest whether to sing them fast or slow.*

Different styles of music are characterized by particular approaches. For example, the typically laid-back feel of a blues song is achieved by singing predominantly behind the beat. In faster rock music you might sing slightly ahead of the beat to drive the music forward and add to the excitement.

Many people focus only on the sound they are producing when they work on their singing. However, rhythm is a vital element too. A singer can sing the most beautiful melody but if they have a poor sense of rhythm the song becomes lifeless and will not engage the listener.

This is just as important in classical singing. Indeed, I heard Bryn Terfyl, the wonderful Welsh baritone, say that Sir George Solti once punched the rhythm of a piece out so hard on his arm that it left him with bruises. It further goes to show how you sometimes have to suffer for your art!

Take things one step at a time. When you start to feel more comfortable with the rhythm and phrasing, you can experiment and try taking 'risks' with the melody.

Ideally, you should know the original tune inside out before you start to move away from it. Many people think they know a song well, but it is only when they come to sing it without any help from the original that they discover they don't. They may only have a 'sketchy' idea, perhaps only really knowing a couple of lines of a verse and most of the chorus.

> *Now sing a line. Hold the last note and move it up, then try again, moving down. It's simple really. Just choose another note that fits with the chord. Altering the last note of a phrase is probably the most common form of improvisation.*

Even if you don't understand the harmonic structure of a song, by listening closely and singing along to it, you will be able to work out which notes fit with the chords and which don't. The more secure you have the chord structure and harmony in your head the better.

> *If you play piano or guitar, play the chords from a familiar song. Sing the melody. Now start on a mid-range note. Try to sing all the words on this one note. When you change chord, if this note doesn't fit, try moving it up or down just one semitone or tone. Go through the song, keeping the movement this economical. In this way you get right 'inside' the harmony of a song.*
>
> *Now sing the verse and alter the end of each line, making up your own tune to fit with the chords. Extend this to the chorus and the other verses. You are now improvising.*

Another great way to practice is to play a blues progression and sing over it. Start with short phrases, just a few notes, gradually extending the rhythmic patterns and melody. This type of improvisation should feel like a musical journey or story, with a beginning, a middle and an end.

Because blues songs are based around a simple harmonic pattern, they are very good vehicles for improvisation. Anybody who has improvised blues on the guitar or piano, for example, will identify with what I said earlier about the excitement created by 'sitting behind the beat' and 'pushing'. In fact, a singer's improvisations quite often imitate guitar lines – for example, when 'bending' notes.

Good improvisation relies on a solid technique. The more adventurous you become, the more flexible your voice will have to be. Changing between registers will have to be smooth, for example.

But improvisation is not a question of pure inspiration: largely, the ideas upon which it is based can be found in the melody, lyrics and instrumentation of the song.

Often it is structured around instrumental ideas found in a song, such as guitar or piano riffs. Small, improvised ideas based on these would be used more as fillers or ad libs, in instrumental sections or at the end of a song. They are usually sung on sounds such as 'mm', 'ah', 'oh' or 'whoah' with the singer using their voice like an instrument (for example, by bending and sliding).

There are endless other forms of improvisation. A singer might choose at times to drop the lead and improvise over the backing vocals. They might 'answer' a BV (backing vocal). At other times a singer might select only a few words from the chorus to work with and add their own variations.

In an outro (the end section of a song), an experienced singer will take short musical excursions in which they will develop some of the original phrases and introduce new musical ideas – often with strong, repeated, rhythmic patterns. These might involve sounds rather than words. A clichéd imported lyric such as 'baby ... I say baby', still works amazingly well, largely because it is there for rhythmic rather than lyrical effect.

For jazz improvisation you can start by trying many of the things above. This is how I learned. As you get more advanced you need to know about the different scales and modes, but that is beyond the scope of this particular book.

Nobody really sings songs totally 'straight'. This is largely because everybody has been influenced by the singers they listen to and like. Often without realizing, they have taken on board all sorts of stylistic embellishments. In fact, listening to the phrasing and stylistic effects of the singers you like is the best thing you can do. If you don't feel confident about improvising, it is a great idea to start by copying the improvisations of those who are good at it. As your own musical vocabulary and confidence grow, the more you will feel the urge to step out on your own. This can be great fun, so get started – you might surprise yourself!

Shredders

This is a term used by guitar players for really flashy, speedy playing. Examples of 'shredders' are Eddie Van Halen and Steve Vai. They have practiced technique for hours and hours to get themselves up to virtuoso standard. The agility and dexterity that they display is awesome. There are also singers for whom this is the case.

Many R&B singers are particularly known for their vocal agility and the effect can be very exciting (if it isn't overdone). Beyoncé Knowles is a great example, flashing up and down with her sparkling R&B licks.

One of the most agile (and golden) voices I have come across is Craig David's. I was lucky enough to work with Craig when he did his first two tours. Craig is obviously someone not desperately in need of singing coaching. He certainly has a remarkable natural talent and he just needed help with minor aspects of technique and stamina management that would allow him to preserve his voice while on an arduous tour. (He still takes really good care of his voice, and I'm glad to say he took my advice and always warms up properly before every performance.)

As part of a warm-up and as a means of strengthening the voice I use fast-moving articulation exercises. I have never known a voice to move as quickly as Craig's. I could not possibly keep up with him on the piano. Not only does his voice move ridiculously quickly, but every single note is absolutely spot on in pitch and very even in tone. His flexibility and accuracy are quite extraordinary. He is truly, in the best sense, a 'shredder' of the vocal world.

Not many voices are capable of moving as quickly as Craig David's. He has an extremely light, agile voice; other singers have weightier voices. Take Elton John or Bono for example. Their voices are heavier and they wouldn't sound right doing fast riffs. It's no coincidence that their voices suit their material.

However, if you work at it you can improve agility and I shall be giving you some exercises to help later in the book.

R&B Licks

R&B music is an extremely popular form and is responsible for attracting a lot of people into singing. Many singers who come to me want, in particular, to improve their agility and their 'riffing' or 'licks'.

The best way to work on this is to listen closely to an artist that you admire and try to copy their 'licks'. Don't be over-ambitious. Choose one lick at a time. Listen to it several times; then try repeating it. Slow it down. If that is not working, sketch it out. You can do this by drawing a line that follows the shape of the lick. Does it go up or down, start high then go low, etc.?

To get the flexibility you need for the riffs, the sound has to be placed forward. Remember, this means thinking of the sound ringing around the front of your face and head. If your voice is too open at the back, there will be too much weight in it and you won't be able to get it moving quickly enough.

Getting to be good at riffing is really down to practice. Many singers appear to be naturally good at it. This is because they have listened to a lot of R&B music and have learned the 'language'. There is no doubt that you can improve your riffing if you work at it, although some singers will find it more difficult than others because of the type of voice they have.

R&B And The Gospel Tradition

Many R&B singers borrow from the great Gospel-singing tradition whose own roots lie in traditional African music and the spirituals and black church music arising from the slavery era in the United States. The origins and significance of Gospel music are complex but many take the work of Mahalia Jackson and her contemporaries in the 1940s and 50s as the starting point of modern black Gospel singing.

While they may be hard to define in simple terms, the black Gospel sound and style are instantly recognizable. The singing features great emotional intensity, as one would expect from a form of music inextricably linked to a declaration of black selfhood and passionate Christian spirituality and faith.

It also features extravagant improvisation or ornamentation. There is often a 'call and answer' between the soloist and the choir (or the preacher and his congregation), echoing traditional black 'field' and working songs. Incidentally, you often hear this 'call and answer' in popular singing, especially the Blues, and particularly within improvised 'BV's.

Of course, though religious in origin, Gospel music has exerted a great deal of influence on today's popular music forms and styles. Indeed, soul music was one of the earliest popular forms that was heavily influenced by Gospel music. A large number of leading soul artists began their musical careers as Gospel singers, or accompanists in Baptist, Methodist and Pentecostal churches. The list includes, among others, James Brown, Aretha Franklin, Ray Charles, Lou Rawls, Sam Cooke and Otis Redding.

The Gospel singing style is a performer's art. It is a method of delivering lyrics so demanding in vocal skill and technique that its performing process, like that of the jazz musician, is highly spontaneous and intuitive in approach. In other words, not everyone can do it!

The ornamentation used by Gospel singers seems to me totally appropriate to the form and spiritual sentiment of the music being expressed. What matters is a down-to-earth sincerity and heart-felt identification with the message of the song or hymn. My own view, however, is that, whilst its influence on popular R&B singing cannot be denied, adopting the ornamentation, style and phrasing of spiritual and Gospel singing without its technical expertise and sensitivity, can result in a kind of 'phoney' or shallow style of singing – what I call 'style over substance'.

Style-Over-Substance Singing

This approach to singing has unfortunately become very popular, especially among young singers. You only have to listen to the auditionees on shows like *American Idol, Pop Idol* or *Fame Academy.* In an attempt to impress the judges, many of them try to add as many 'licks' as possible. To be fair, the auditionees normally only have a very short time in which to catch the eyes and ears of the judges and so the temptation is understandable.

I also think some of the blame for this can be directed towards a few of the top R&B artists themselves. I have noticed an increasing tendency to overdo the riffing within a song to a point where the original melody of the song is rarely referred to. My view is that whilst this is fine, say, in the context of modern improvised jazz, it can be overdone in R&B singing, where I like to hear the original melodic heart of a song (especially a good one) coming through.

When I worked on *Popstars The Rivals* this was a real bugbear for the judges. One of my main jobs, more so with the boys than the girls, was to teach them a song and get them to sing the melody, in order that we could really hear the quality of their voices – something that proved difficult when they had come determined to 'go off on one' in a style-over-substance kind of a way! They had to learn the melody and get that right before they were allowed to put their own mark on the song.

Unfortunately, many singers determined to sing in this way also happen to sing completely out of tune and/or have no idea about improvising around the chords of the song. This style of singing can also disguise poor technique and lack of breath control. Phrases can be very clipped, the singing very 'breathy', and all too often the singers are incapable of sustaining notes of any length.

Style-over-substance singers appeal to those who are fooled into thinking or, should we say, are prepared to believe that fancy licks and agility equal great singing. These singers have all the 'style' of a particular genre – the phrasing and licks, for example – or what you might call the 'surface' features. But, sadly, many have no real technique, musical line, emotional quality or genuine musicality – all the things that are ultimately rewarding to the listener. When I hear their vocal pyrotechnics I am always reminded of the old phrase, *never mind the quality, feel the width*.

I believe in getting 'inside' and finding a person's individual or 'real' voice, discovering what makes them tick, and bringing out their own individual qualities when they sing. All successful artists with any longevity have a real identity that 'speaks' to you. This comes from within. It is not something that is 'painted on'.

It is important, of course, to have freedom in your singing and to have your own style. Bringing your own inflections to a melody will bring it to life. Indeed, as I have said before, it would be boring if singers stuck rigidly to the melody all the way through a song. However, improvising should be an organic process, and the results should be meaningful and musical – not just a matter of fitting in as many notes as possible in order to impress.

Cadenzas

Ornamentation has been used to decorate and embellish music for many years. The cadenza is the name given to a brilliant solo passage performed by a solo voice or instrumentalist. It appears near the end of an aria or movement of a concerto. It is a great showpiece for singers. It was introduced by Italian opera singers in the late seventeenth century and soon after that in Germany. The original idea was that it should last no longer than a single breath and should end with a trill.

CHAPTER 14 SUMMARY

- Some singers are natural improvisers, but there are many aspects of improvisation that you can learn.

- You can start by experimenting with changes in the rhythm and phrasing of a song and then go on to varying the melody.

- Many of the ideas upon which improvisation is based can be found in the melody, lyrics and instrumentation of the song.

- To get the flexibility you need for agile R&B riffs, the sound has to be placed forward.

- Guard against adopting the ornamentation, style and phrasing of Gospel singing unless you have the technique to do it justice.

- Your own improvisation should be meaningful and musical – not just a matter of fitting in as many notes as possible in order to impress.

Chapter 15
Tuning

Am I Tone Deaf?

I constantly hear people being written off as singers by others – and equally often by themselves – on the grounds that they are irredeemably 'tone deaf'.

Many people are so hung up about this that they rarely, and sometimes never, sing in case someone hears and laughs at them. The sad fact is that many of these people have a secret desire to be singers. I believe it is really unfair and damaging to make fun of someone's singing. In addition, I would like to say a few things about out-of-tune singing and explain why there might yet be hope for even the most extreme cases.

There are a number of reasons why people have tuning problems but they often derive from negative childhood or teenage experiences. Many adults I know don't sing because at the age of seven or eight they were not chosen for the school choir, or were teased and made to believe they had hopeless voices. This has been enough to put them off for life.

It is true, unfortunately, that some people do have a problem singing in tune – and some more than others. As I said, there are many reasons for this and they may not be quite what you would expect.

The term 'tone deaf' is a little harsh (I prefer, as you know, 'singing like a dog' – no, only joking). The expression is used to describe a singer who sings totally and consistently out of tune – something which in actual fact is quite a difficult thing to achieve: invariably even the worst cases seem to hit some of the notes some of the time.

The expression 'tone deaf' would itself seem to suggest something fixed and unalterable, since, surely, if you are deaf there is nothing you can do about it. However, in my experience, even the most seemingly hopeless cases can be rescued. It may take some time, but it is achievable!

Most people have a reasonable sense of pitch. Commonly, however, some will sing out of tune when trying to sing either too high or low. They can be bang in tune in the middle of their voice, but as they move up or down their voice begins to tense up. The muscles around the larynx clamp down and prevent the vocal cords from vibrating freely to produce the correct pitch. With the right technique these singers can learn to remove this tension. As a result they can begin to sing more reliably in tune whatever the pitch.

Some people start off a song on the right note but go 'wild' as it progresses. This is usually due to their lack of musical experience. For singers like this I recommend they take up an instrument as this will help to train their ears to listen properly. (I don't mean *instead* of singing, of course!)

If you can pick out a simple melody on a keyboard, singing along with the tune will reinforce your sense of pitch. Those who can play chords may extend this by singing their own tunes around the chords. Make sure you are singing notes that fit with the chord you are playing and don't clash. It may sound obvious, but believe me many people don't do it!

There are also physical reasons why people sing out of tune. Some adults have never really sung and their 'singing muscles' are a bit 'flabby' so it can take some time to tone them up. Other causes include unwanted tension in the jaw area, or 'collapsing' of the body (see pages 35-40). As we have seen before, how you use your body affects your voice and with some people the effect on tuning can be severe.

For some reason, people who have difficulties singing in tune often have a poor sense of rhythm too. An old friend of mine was one such person. Giving up all hope of a singing career, he joined the army and couldn't even march in time!

The most challenging case I ever had was that of a woman in her early thirties. She had an exceptionally deep voice and had experienced many vocal problems. She had a range of only a 3rd (three notes) and produced a sort of 'droning' sound as she attempted to move up and down the scale. There was a huge amount of tension surrounding her jaw, throat, chest and shoulders. We began with songs that had a small range and with very careful and gradual work, she increased her range to an octave and a half, and her tuning became very good. She also learnt an instrument at the same time and this really helped her. She may never be an amazing singer but she can hold a tune and make a perfectly acceptable sound – and she loves it!

Due to vocal misuse some very good singers can find themselves developing tuning problems. The upsetting thing is that they can hear they are singing out of tune but can do little to change it. They have to either push their voices, particularly in the upper middle part, or sing very quietly to get the pitch anywhere near accurate. This kind of problem is often a warning sign of the development of nodules (see page 164). If this is happening, I would seriously recommend having a check-up and singing lessons from a good teacher.

Perfect Pitch

This is the term used for certain people's ability to recognize and name a note on first hearing. People with perfect pitch can also sing any note within their range unaccompanied.

I have perfect pitch and it is something I think I was born with. You are unlikely to know you have perfect pitch unless you have learned an instrument. Having it can be useful, but, as I will explain, not always. It is certainly no indication as to whether you are musical or not (obviously though, it is in my case!), or whether you are a good singer.

It does, however, seem to develop in relation to the instrument you play. I play the piano and could tell you any note on the piano with 100% success. However, my pitch is not quite as reliable with stringed instruments, which suggests there is certainly also a learned element.

The disadvantage comes when you are sight-reading music. Generally speaking, having perfect pitch helps you, but if the key changes you have to start transposing (put the music into another key) on the spot. This has happened to me in the past when I have been singing something quite complex with a group, unaccompanied. As a piece progresses the pitch might drop a tone or so, I then end up having to transpose as I am reading it. It can be scary!

Don't worry if you don't have perfect pitch, neither do most professional singers.

Relative Pitch

On the other hand, most musicians have this. Relative pitch is the ability to pitch notes from a given starting note. In other words, you can hear the relationship between the notes of a melody (the intervals) and be able to sing 'in tune with yourself' from any given starting point. Relative pitch is learned through practice. People who sing regularly, even though they may not have perfect pitch, will eventually develop a feel for whether they are in the right key or on the right note.

Singing In Tune

So how important is it to be able to sing in tune consistently? I imagine most of you would agree with me and reply 'very', but you might be surprised how many arguments I have with people in the music business about this. In fact, the widespread acceptance of poor tuning in the rock and pop world inevitably draws me into a more general discussion about standards of singing. It is my contention that, while there are clearly many absolutely superb singing artists and acts out there, singing standards in rock and pop could and should be much better.

Apart from a general lack of technique that results in weak, breathy, unsustained and 'unconnected' singing, many singers just can't consistently sing in tune. Poor tuning is definitely more accepted in rock and pop than it is in, say, jazz, show or classical singing. Yet it is interesting to note that in no other area of rock and pop musicianship would these lax standards be tolerated.

Having said that, I appreciate that when singing live, there are often genuine reasons for bad tuning. For example, singers often have difficulty hearing themselves on stage, usually for reasons to do with the P.A. or other factors beyond their control. I also agree that a certain amount of out-of-tune singing is acceptable within the context of a live rock and pop performance, where, 'feel' and excitement take priority.

Overall, however, I think the ability to sing in tune is a basic requirement of any singer. Nobody should expect perfect tuning all the time – the vast majority of singers will not hit every single note of a song bang on (although the best ones can hear when they are slightly off and make quick adjustments), but consistently out-of-tune singing is clearly unacceptable.

The reasons for the continued acceptance of poor vocal standards (including poor tuning) and a related resistance to vocal coaching are complex and varied.

On one hand there has always been a view in the business that 'you can either do it or you can't'. Whilst no one can deny there is some truth in this – the Mick Jaggers, Tina Turners and Bonos of this world were clearly 'born to do it' – these huge stars and others like them are in the minority.

It is also worth emphasizing that aside from the fact that these people can sing, much of their success derives from their undoubted personal charisma and stage presence. I would add that these big stars all sing and have always sung live regularly and very much in tune! The rest of us mere mortals will benefit from working on our technique – and tuning.

The importance of image and looks in contemporary pop music, boosted by the popularity of 'fame wannabes' shows, has led to a crop of singers who, not to put too fine a point on it, have little in the way of technique and often an inability to sing in tune consistently.

What sets the 'genuine' artists apart from the others is their ability to sing and perform live. Many of the 'created' artists rely heavily on studio production and techniques to hide their technical inadequacies.

A classic example, in the context of a discussion on tuning, is the over-reliance in studios on digitally tuning recorded vocals. Producers can now 'tune' an out-of-tune vocal when the singer has long gone home and is tucked up in bed. I think this is fine for minor adjustments, but if the whole vocal has to be treated in this way (and it does happen frequently) you begin to wonder why they bothered in the first place.

It begs the question, if a singer has to rely on this kind of equipment to sing in tune in the 'ideal' environment of a recording studio, what chance do they have of singing on the note in a live situation?

Some people are content to be 'studio stars'; the rest of us want the much greater buzz of singing well in front of an audience.

What Key Do I Sing In?

This is something people ask me all the time. It sounds a perfectly logical question, but in fact it doesn't make any sense. Let me explain.

You can sing in *any* key – it just depends on where the melody you want to sing lies within that key. In other words the highest or lowest notes of the song must be within your range.

Take for example the key of C major. The notes in the scale are C, D, E, F, G, A, B, and C. In G major, the notes of the scale are G, A, B, C, D, E, F sharp and G. You can see from this that both scales share the same notes, except that G has an F sharp where C has an F.

All the major and minor scales share the same notes, except the sharps and flats vary depending on the key that you are in.

Whether you can sing a song in any one key depends on which notes are in the tune and how high (or low) they go. A high B or G may make the song too high for you. A tune that only uses mid-range Bs and Gs would be easier to sing. As you can see from the examples, these notes appear in both the G and C scales. Therefore, it doesn't make sense to say, 'I can only sing in G, not C.'

If a song has a high B or G and you can only manage a high E or C you will need to transpose or lower the key of the song by a 5th. This would take the B down to E and the G down to C.

Alternatively, if the low notes of a song are too low you would need to transpose up. If the lowest note you feel comfortable singing is a D and the lowest note of the song is a low A, you would need to raise the key by a 4th.

Keys are funny things. Some songs just don't sound right sung in certain keys – we know from experience, for example, that some keys sound naturally 'brighter' than others.

In addition, many musicians write songs in C and G, since the common (open) chords in these keys are familiar. G is a common and important note in both these keys. The problem many singers have is that a high G is just about at the top of their range. Choruses in these two keys, particularly, are often written around high Gs and can become very tiring for your voice. I have some suggestions to help you with this.

Obviously, the easiest option for the singer would be to lower the key, but it may well just not be practical for you or the band. If your band is covering or has written and rehearsed a song and has spent ages working out riffs or guitar solos, the last thing you want to have to do is change the key.

The next option is to use alternative melody notes, taking a lower harmony, for example. If you were singing a G over a G chord, you could replace it with a D (the 5th of the chord). Alternatively, if you were singing a G over a C chord, you could replace it with an E (the 3rd of the chord).

I hope this doesn't all sound too mind-boggling – it isn't really. If you play around with these ideas on a keyboard or guitar I think you will soon get the idea.

Another way around it is to sing in falsetto. Now, I know, as previously intimated, many people think falsetto singing is a weaker-sounding option, but if you have a bunch of harmonies going on as well, it can sound really good. An additional advantage of using falsetto is that it will help prevent you from wrecking your voice! You will probably never get your falsetto as strong as your head voice, but with practice you can get it sounding pretty good.

Singing High

Correct use of head voice is the real answer to sustaining a high melody. As we have seen, the problem many of you will have is taking your chest voice too high. Remember, *chest voice* is the term used to describe the place you resonate the sound when you sing lower notes. As you sing up the scale, the feeling of the resonance should move gradually into your head (*head voice*). If you don't allow this to happen, you will 'push' the top of your voice too much, eventually leading to strain (see *Registers,* page 61).

Don't forget, if you do transpose a song down and sing it in a lower key than the original, it doesn't mean you are a poorer singer. Some people simply have higher or lower voices than others.

CHAPTER 15 SUMMARY

- A certain amount of out-of-tune singing is acceptable, especially when singing live, but consistently out of tune singing needs to be addressed.

- There are a number of reasons why people may have tuning problems, but something can be done about most of them.

- Perfect pitch is the ability to instantly recognize and name a played note, or the ability to sing any named note accurately.

- Relative Pitch is the ability to pitch notes from a given starting note.

- Theoretically, you can sing in *any* key, so long as the highest or lowest notes of the particular song are within your range.

- Correct use of head voice is the real answer to sustaining a high melody.

Chapter 16
Singing Exercises

Why Do Singing Exercises?

Working with singing exercises is an integral part of any program designed to develop a good singing technique. Whatever style of music you sing, they are the linchpins.

Having said that, I am afraid many so-called singing coaches use singing exercises in an entirely arbitrary way, often without understanding in what way a particular exercise might be helping the singer. Furthermore, I have heard of numerous examples over the years of ridiculous exercises (beware, especially, those trying to appear 'trendy' or 'witty') whose worth is completely lost on me.

For these reasons I have added notes to the recommended exercises below that aim to explain their usefulness.

If you apply all the main principles I have outlined in this book, your singing will really improve. However, working with singing exercises will not only help you develop your voice; it will also help you gain a real awareness of how you should be using it.

There are many benefits to be gained from working with singing exercises regularly. These include: improving breath control; strengthening your voice; increasing your range; developing your tone and resonance; gaining understanding and control of your registers; and increasing vocal agility.

Practicing singing exercises regularly helps to develop appropriate *muscle memory*. The muscles involved in singing are used to responding, or are in the habit of responding, in certain ways when we sing. Some of the things they do may be technically undesirable: an example of this is the way our jaw and tongue muscles sometimes set up unwanted tensions that adversely affect our singing. The idea of singing exercises is to stimulate your 'good' muscles to work.

Different exercises work on different aspects of technique. As you practice, you are training your muscles to respond in a technically healthy way and, given time, the old muscles will 'let go'.

Many singers worry that if they do singing exercises they will start to sound like opera singers. Obviously some of you will *want* to sound like opera singers and that is great. If you *don't* want to sound like an opera singer, don't worry: you are the one in control of the sound you make (through the choices you make about resonance, phrasing, etc.) and it is more accurate to regard the benefits of singing exercises as giving you *more* choices.

The intention is for your voice to develop into a strong, stable instrument with which you can 'play' any kind of music. Remember, virtually all kinds of singing rely on the same basic principles of technique. As you develop your voice, you will be able to do more things with it – an exciting thought.

Some singers initially find the thought of practicing with singing exercises quite daunting. It can feel totally alien to use their voices in such an ordered way, having always sung instinctively before. If you are one of these, don't be put off. Persevere with the exercises and you really will see the benefits. Don't expect to do them perfectly at first. In fact, it doesn't matter how long you've been singing – you can always get a bit more out of an exercise. You can never stop learning.

It is better to go through exercises with an experienced teacher if you can, as he or she will ensure that you are not doing anything wrong. This, however, is a self-help book, so I am going to give you detailed notes on how to approach the exercises on your own. This will help you to get the best out of them and ensure that you only improve and don't run the risk of damaging your voice.

Exercises can also be used as a warm-up. If you are using them for this purpose, don't do too many and make sure you pace yourself. Five or ten minutes may be enough (see *Warm Up*, page 169). You can do them in any order. Different things suit different people.

The exercises I am giving you are very much a selection. There are many more, but these are a good start. I am going to begin with some general humming exercises and then move on to more specifically technical ones. In the general warm-up section I have set out some exercises that you can do without the help of an instrument.

The exercises I am going to give you in this section are based around musical notation. If you don't read music, get a friend who plays keyboard or guitar (or any other suitable instrument) to record the basic shapes for you on tape so you can then practice them as much as you like. Many people I know practice to tapes in their cars, which is okay, but ideally, you should be standing.

All the suggestions for starting notes are very general. Start where you feel comfortable – it will vary depending on voice type. Remember never to try to go too high or low. You shouldn't strain your voice doing exercises. Some singers like to start their exercises high and descend. You can choose which way feels best for you. It is suggested in each exercise that you move in semitones (half steps) up or down.

All of the exercises (except for the humming) are sung on vowel sounds. The reason for this is, as I have said before, the singing sound only happens on the vowels and not the consonants (see *Singing On The Vowel*, page 80).

Sing the exercises at medium volume, unless otherwise instructed. Don't sing them constantly at the top of your voice; it will become too tiring. Sometimes you will want to let rip, and indeed it can be hard to get the support going at first if the singing is too quiet.

The order of these exercises is unimportant. Some will suit you more than others. Don't try all of them at once. Start with a few and gradually introduce some more. Some singers prefer to start with the articulation exercises as they get your voice moving – but it's really up to you.

My Top Twenty Singing Exercises

Each of the following twenty exercises is given in the key of C with the intention that they should be transposed as appropriate for your voice type. Suggestions for starting notes are given under each exercise. Simply repeat the exercise, transposing up a semitone each time until you reach the limit of your range, or the upper limit that I suggest in the text, whichever is lower.

1. Humming

This is a good, gentle warm-up. Hum up and down a five-note scale passage. Don't take it too high.

Men: Start around B flat (an octave and a bit below middle C). Only go as high as A or B below middle C.

Women: The same as for men but an octave higher.

2. Five-note Scale Passage

This exercise encourages you to sing with more space in the back of your throat.

It uses the same pattern as above but on an 'oh'.

To start with, do this in the same register as exercise 1. As you sing the exercise, think of having a round, open space in the back of your throat. Imagine you are filling your body with sound.

You can repeat this on 'ah' and 'ee'. If it helps, put an 'm' sound in front of the vowel – this helps to 'trigger' the muscles you use to support your voice.

3. Triads

This exercise encourages singing with an open throat and a low larynx.

Sing this exercise in the same register as exercises 1 and 2. As you sing, imagine a see-saw moving down as the singing goes up. Keep an open space in the back of your throat. Sing it on 'oh', 'ah' and 'ee'.

As you get more familiar with this you can extend it throughout your voice. It is a good one for opening up the chest. Always be aware that as you go higher you gradually have to sing with more head resonance.

4. Repeated Notes

This exercise has a number of benefits: it helps to tone up your vocal cords by getting them to come together properly, enabling you to start a note cleanly; it also helps to eliminate unwanted breathiness; and it is great for putting you in touch with your support muscles and getting the sound flowing through your body.

Do this exercise in the lower to middle part of your range.

Men: Start on D or D flat below middle C, up in semitones to E, and then back down.

Women: Sing the same as the men but an octave higher.

Sing these repeated notes first on 'oh', 'ah' and then 'ee'. This is a tricky exercise to get to grips with. Don't be tempted to sneak extra breath in; it should be sung in one breath. The exercise should flow from beginning to end, even though you keep stopping the sound. The key is to make sure the onset of each note is not 'glottal' – that means it shouldn't feel like it is starting from your throat: it should feel like you are leaning into the note. You lean down on the column of air. There is almost a feeling of resistance, but the sound moves further down the singing tube with each note.

You can imagine that the singing starts in your tummy. Have your hands here as you sing and feel the tummy coming in with each note. Keep the muscle tension going in between each note; don't let your support go 'sloppy'. Also, be careful not to let any air out before the start of each note.

I use this exercise a lot, particularly if I've had a lay off due to a cold or cough. It is great for everyone, but especially those with any voice problems.

5.   Staccato Arpeggio

This exercise uses the same principles as the last. It works on support and the prevention of 'glottal attack'. Again you shouldn't feel the onset of each note in your throat. As you go up, think down. Think of a lift moving down, or a cafetière plunging down as you sing up. Make sure you pull (or spring) in from your tummy and support the upper note.

Men: begin on B an octave and a bit below middle C. Stop around E.

Women: The same range as men but an 8ve higher.

Make sure the singing feels 'connected' all the time. If it feels strained or pushed, stop. Staccato exercises can be very beneficial but they are hard work and require lots of support.

Try it on 'oh', 'ah' and 'ee'.

6.   Legato Arpeggio

This arpeggio exercise will help in smoothing out the transition from one register to another and give you a greater awareness of your registers – where they change and the differences between them. It also helps with both support and keeping a low larynx.

Think down as you sing up the scale. Sing it on 'oh', 'ah' and 'ee'. You may want to put a 'm' before each vowel to help you to anchor your support (making 'moh', 'mah' and 'mee').

Keep the support going. Think of a combination of a downward movement and a pull in from your tummy a split second before you sing the high note. This gives you more chance to get the support and low larynx working together.

As you go higher, allow the sound to move gradually into your head. It may help you to think of it getting lighter. You should encourage the introduction of head voice into the sound.

Start this in the same place as the previous exercise. Take it as high as feels comfortable. As you go higher open your mouth more. If it helps, put your fingers in the 'groove' (see page 31) and make sure your soft palate is lifting with a little inner 'smile'.

As you take the sound higher, allow the resonance to come into the front of your head, but always keep the space open in the back of your throat. It seems a bit confusing at first, as you have to think in two directions simultaneously. Modify the vowels so 'ah' and 'oh' become more 'awe' (a bit yawny in the back of your throat – without pushing down your tongue) and 'ee' becomes more 'i' (as in 'lid'). This will help to keep your larynx relaxed and give more depth to the sound.

7.   Arpeggio Plus Dominant 7th

This exercise is another good one for linking up the registers. It is also a useful 'ear trainer' as the descending pattern is slightly unpredictable.

Focus on the same elements of technique as you did in the previous exercise. Some people find this easier than the arpeggio as it is a bit freer-flowing.

Use the same range as above.

8.   Arpeggio Plus 10th

This is a slightly extended version of the arpeggio exercises. Sing it fairly quickly. I recommend the fingers in the 'groove' for this one.

Use the same range and vowels as before.

9.   Extended Arpeggio Plus Dominant 7th

This exercise is similar to the other arpeggio-based ones. It stretches you a bit further and it requires good control to be accurate on the way down.

Make sure you open up at the top.

Sing on the same vowels as in the previous exercise and start in the same place. Take it as high as is comfortable.

10.   Five-note Scales And Triad Combined

This is a particularly good exercise for breath control, as it should last for about eight seconds in total. It also helps with the transition from one register to another and with the development, in particular, of your middle register. You can sing it on 'oh', 'ah', 'ee' and 'oo'.

Start off singing in the middle of your voice. In time you can take it throughout your whole voice and it is a great strengthener. Don't open your mouth too wide at the bottom. Keep the sound 'focused' but still keep the space in the back of your throat.

Men: Start around C below middle C. Take it up to about a G, so your highest note would be D. If it feels comfortable you can take it higher. You will need to introduce more head voice into the sound. When you get to E or E flat you should be singing with more head voice and by the time you've reached F/F sharp it should be right in your head.

Women: Start in the same place as men but an octave higher. Allow the sound to begin moving into your head around E flat/E. You will then be singing with a mix of chest and head registers, which is known as your middle register. As you go higher let the sound go more into your head. In the middle you want a real mix of chest and head registers.

Some singers find this exercise easier if they start higher and descend.

11. Held Single Notes

This exercise works on resonance and tone production. It also encourages you to be relaxed as you sing – both with your breath and in your body.

Sing a single mid- to low-range note and hold it for the length of your breath. As you hold it, feel the resonance (buzz) ringing around the front of your face. Sing on 'ooh' and then 'ee'.

Men: Start on F below middle C and descend in semitones.

Women: Start an octave higher.

12. Five-note Run And Hold

This is an extension of the previous exercise and works on both resonance and forward placing.

You can start by doing the first example and work up to the second one. Sing it on 'ooh', 'ee', 'oh' and 'ah'. The range is the same as in the previous exercise.

13.   Five-note Run And Hold With Vowel Bend

This exercise works on resonance, placing and vowel unification (moving from one vowel to another smoothly).

This is the same as the previous exercise, although as you hold the note you move from 'ee' to 'ai' to 'ah'. It is quite hard to do this smoothly. Don't move from one sound to the other by changing your mouth shape; alter them inside. You do it by lifting the stretchy soft palate. Each vowel should grow out of the previous one; there should not be any sudden gear changes. Use the same range as above.

14.   Rotating The Registers

This is an exercise for women. It is designed to help develop an awareness of the difference between chest voice and middle register and to smooth out the changes. Sing the first three notes in chest voice and then the fourth note in middle register, ending the exercise in chest voice. The change to middle register is hard as you will have already sung the upper note in chest the first time. As you move into mixed register, think down. This will help you to keep your larynx low and relaxed. Also think of making the sound a bit lighter.

Start on middle C and descend in semitones (half steps) to the A flat below. Then come back up. As you practice this exercise you can gradually reduce the size of the interval you are singing from a major third to a second. For example you start off rotating from C to E, then sing C to E flat, then C to D. This will help you to develop control.

15. Octave Jumps – Rotating The Registers

This is another good one for women. It is quite an advanced exercise; be careful not to overdo things. You sing the lower notes in chest voice or mixed register and the upper notes in head voice.

Always remember to think down and support as you sing up.
Start on middle C ascending in semitones (half steps). Stop on the F or F sharp above.

Each time you sing the upper note you will have to allow for an increasing amount of head resonance in the sound.

Depending on voice type, the sound will be in your head at C or C sharp above middle C. As you go up, it changes again around F or F sharp as it moves to a higher place in your head.

Men can use this exercise to practice going from full voice into falsetto. Start on F below middle C.

Sing it on 'ooh', 'ee', and 'ah'.

16. Articulation – Scale With Turnaround

This exercise will help you improve your vocal agility. The trick with articulation is that you don't try to sing each note. *Think* the notes as you sing and try not to have too much weight in your voice.

Some people's voices are naturally more agile than others, but you can improve your agility with practice.

Start with your mouth quite focused. It can help a lot if you sing with your fingers in the 'groove'. As you go higher, open your mouth more; keep the space in the back or your throat and allow the sound to go into the front of your head.

Keep the breath low and remember to support the sound, particularly at the top. It helps if you think of a slight emphasis on the first one of every four notes.

Men: Start on B below middle C (if you have a very low voice, start on the G below). Go as high as feels comfortable.

Women: The same range but an octave higher.

Sing on 'ee', 'oh', 'ah' and 'oo'. You may find it easier to put an 'm' before each vowel. This helps to stop you attacking the starting note from your glottis. It softens the onset of the vowel, takes pressure off your vocal cords, and helps to get you connected to the support.

17.   Articulation

This is a similar exercise to the previous one but the patterns are different. You will probably find that the singing feels easier on the way down. The reason for this is that once you have reached the top you will have established your head voice, and then as you descend you will automatically sing with more head voice. On the way up you will tend to drag the chest voice too high if you're not careful. Breathe before descending.

You can think of this exercise as a '1231' pattern, because you sing the 1st note of the scale, then the 2nd, then the 3rd, before returning to the 1st. To take this exercise further you can vary the pattern. Try:
a) 1321 b) 3213 c) 1243
Sing on the same vowels as above, in the same register.

18. Octave Plus Descending Scale

This is a lovely one to sing and, again, is generally better for women.

Follow all the previous instructions for articulation exercises. As you sing the octave leap, think down and support. As you sing the upper notes, swing your arms out to the sides of the room. It gives you a great feeling of freedom as well as making it easier to sing.

Start on middle C and take it as high as is comfortable. Sing on a 'mee' and a 'mah'.

19. Combination Exercise

This is a very advanced exercise that combines some of the previous articulation exercises. It is technically very challenging. Use the same principles, the same vowels, and start on the same notes as in the other articulation exercises. Only do this one if you're really feeling on top of your game!

20. Falsetto Exercises

This is an exercise for men. It will strengthen your falsetto and help to get rid of any unwanted breathiness.

Sing the five-note pattern (from exercise 1) in falsetto. Keep the breath relaxed. You want a feeling of stillness in your body as you sing this. Don't try to force the sound out. Stay calm.

Sing first on 'moo' then 'mee' and 'mah'. Keep the space in the back of your throat, but place the notes very forward in your head and the front of your face around your nose (don't make the sound nasal). Keep your mouth focused.

You may find the 'mah' more difficult and breathy. Keep it focused and try to slot it into the same place as the other vowels.

Start on E above middle C. Ascend in semitones as high as is comfortable, and then come back down.

You can make up other musical patterns based around this five-note exercise to add variety to your falsetto practice. Sing through Radiohead's 'High and Dry' (from their album *The Bends*). It's a great one for linking full voice to falsetto. As you sing the 'high' and 'dry', stretch your arms out wide. It should feel great. Don't reach for the falsetto notes; just let them go naturally into your head as you think down. Stay calm and it should just happen. You could also try singing more on the vowel: 'high' would become 'hah' and 'dry' would become 'drah'.

Finally, when you practice make sure you pace yourself. Don't be too ambitious. Start by selecting a few of the exercises. Remember, different exercises suit different people. Also, some singers prefer singing on the more forward 'ee' and 'oo' vowels, whilst others prefer the open vowels 'oh', 'awe' and 'ah'. It will be helpful to practice all of these exercises in time, but experiment with what feels most comfortable for you and start with those.

Begin by practicing for just five minutes. As you get stronger and understand better what you are doing, you can increase it to ten or fifteen minutes. A practice of this length is absolutely fine for most people. Do thirty minutes maximum. It may not sound much but that is a lot of concentrated singing.

Many singers practice their exercises separately from their repertoire. This can be a good idea, as you won't then end up doing too much singing in one go.

CHAPTER 16 SUMMARY

- Working with singing exercises will not only help you to develop your voice, it will give you a real awareness of how you should be using it.

- The benefits of working with singing exercises regularly include: improving breath control; strengthening your voice; increasing your range; developing your tone and resonance; gaining understanding and control of your registers; and increasing vocal agility.

- Practicing with singing exercises regularly helps to develop appropriate *muscle memory*.

- Working with singing exercises does not have to result in your singing sounding 'operatic' – you still have choices about resonance, style, phrasing, etc.

SECTION FOUR:
AUDITIONING AND PERFORMANCE

The majority of people will buy this book to maximize their own singing pleasure – they are the bathtub Robbies or Pavarottis and the wannabe Whitneys or Kiris. Some of you may want to take your singing one step further and make the transition from lounge to karaoke bar or local stage.

But for those who take their singing even more seriously, and in particular, for those who are considering auditioning for professional singing projects themselves, I include here some practical advice on auditioning techniques and performance.

Chapter 17
Auditioning

If you are serious about auditioning then the first rule is: be fully prepared. Whether it is for a part in a school play, choir, dramatic/operatic society, the West End/Broadway, a pop band or reality TV show, you need to prepare thoroughly. It is vital that you put yourself across in the best possible light, and give clear glimpses of your true potential.

If you haven't prepared fully, this will almost inevitably become evident in the audition, leaving you and the people for whom you are auditioning feeling frustrated and dissatisfied. In some cases, auditionees turn up still not completely sure which song to sing. This gives the impression of a lack of commitment, even if this is not the case. Often it is hard to choose the right song and you need to make sure it is appropriate (see below), but you *must* have decided on something to sing before you go in. Some people will thoroughly prepare two or three songs, giving the panel the final choice.

Virtually all the information given in the *Performance* chapter (see page 129*)* is relevant to the auditioning situation. When you are in an audition it is particularly important to maintain eye contact with the people to whom you are singing. Remember, don't just stare into space; you want to communicate with them when you sing and put across your personality.

This doesn't mean you have to 'eyeball' one person all the way through. There are usually several people in the room, so sing to them all. If they don't want to look, or it makes them feel uncomfortable, they will look away or start writing notes.

A musical director with whom I once worked told me one of the reasons he had employed me for a particular job was that I was the only auditionee who had looked at and communicated with him.

Among other things, you need to work out how you are going to stand, what you are doing with your hands, and whether you are going to move around or tap your foot, etc. A good tip is to rehearse using a mirror. The aim is to avoid looking too self-conscious. Rehearse your song or piece, trying out different things and seeing what looks good. You should appear natural and comfortable.

You do not need a full-on dance routine. Singing and dancing auditions are usually separate. If they like what they hear, you will be asked to dance later.

The more prepared you are, the more you will feel in control. Even rehearse walking into the room – remember, you are allowed to smile; in fact, it is highly recommended!

Finally, make sure you look your best – image is very important. Your hair and clothes should complement the musical idiom the panel is interested in – if the audition is for a pop singer, it would be inappropriate to come as a punk or Madame Butterfly. Wear clothes you feel comfortable in: avoid clothes that restrict your throat or breathing, and don't, for example, decide to sing in high heels if you are not used to it (especially you guys). It is generally not a good idea to dress too outrageously, unless you are totally committed to what you see as your unique look.

Remember, although image will definitely enter into the equation, it is your voice, personality and (depending on the audition) your acting or dancing ability people are interested in.

Choosing Material

If you are auditioning for a specific part in a musical or opera your song choice is obviously pretty straightforward. If you are going for a more general audition for, say, a pop band or even a choir you need to have a selection of material. Make a firm decision before you go as to what you are going to sing. Ideally, take two songs (or pieces) with you. Decide which is your best and start with that. If they want to hear more, you have got it with you.

You must learn your songs thoroughly. Choose one up-tempo number and a ballad by way of contrast. If you are singing classical music, choose two contrasting pieces, perhaps one in a foreign language.

Depending on the type of audition, you may not get to sing a song the whole way through. The more auditionees there are, the less time you will have to impress the listener.

Sometimes you will be asked for just a verse and a chorus of one song, but it is always good to have more up your sleeve should you be asked for it. It may be felt, for example, that your first song does not suit your voice or show its full potential.

Choose songs that you can sing well, and don't be overambitious. Depending on how experienced a singer you are, it might be an idea to avoid songs with too wide a range – a song that goes too high or low.

It is probably best to steer clear of songs by virtuoso artists such as Whitney Houston, Christina Aguilera and Stevie Wonder (unless you are also amazing, of course!) as most people can't really do them justice. Also, there is nothing more embarrassing than someone trying to reproduce other people's licks and doing it badly. Believe me, I have heard plenty and it's not pleasant!

You want your individuality and personality to come across. A good tip is to choose a song that the panel won't have already heard fifty times that week. At the same time, I wouldn't recommend choosing something *too* quirky or too much outside the mainstream.

If you are singing with an accompanist, be nice to them. If you are not nice, they can give you a tough time! Make sure that the piece is not fiendishly difficult – some accompanists are better readers than others. Make sure you have a copy of the music for the accompanist in the right key. If you are singing in a different key to the sheet music, ensure the chords of the key in which you want to sing are clearly written in. Ideally, have a proper chord chart or specially transposed version (music teachers will often do this for you). Sticky-tape the music together in such a way as to ensure there aren't any tricky page turns. This will also help to guard against the music falling off the piano mid-song!

Confession time: A number of years ago I was playing the piano for some auditions for a musical. Unbeknown to the auditionees I was also at the time the musical director of the project.

One rather pushy-looking girl came in with a piece of music I can only describe as a nightmare. Now, I am no Ashkenazy but I am a pretty good sight-reader. However, I had never seen the like of this piece before. It had numerous changes of time and key. I freely admit that I made a bit of a hash of it. Rather than seeing the funny side she insulted me, saying that other pianists had been able to play it perfectly well before. Needless to say she totally blew her chances of singing another song. I moved swiftly on to the sight-reading – and you can probably guess what kind of piece I chose for her. I'm not normally vindictive, I assure you, but I guess if the story teaches us anything, it is that you should always treat people with respect and good manners – whoever they might be.

Learning The Song

Make sure you know the words inside out, as nerves often make your mind go blank, and if you feel a little unsure you can guarantee you will dry up. If you have difficulty remembering lyrics, write them out. Learn line one, then lines one and two, then lines one, two and three, etc. Often the links between verses cause problems. Giving yourself a mental picture or 'hook' based on the words can help you remember how one verse leads on from the other.

Singing along with the original song is the best way to learn the tune accurately. Learn it a line at a time, just as you did with the lyrics. When you know one verse inside out, sing it without the track. You may think you have got it, but when you take the backing away it can be surprisingly difficult. You begin to realize how much your singing is guided and scaffolded by the original.

Many singers learn a song completely straight – singing it with the same phrasing the whole way through. Like the experienced artist, you should aim to vary things a little. Pay close attention to detail – where the melody changes, for example, or where there are variations in verses, in the middle eights, choruses, ad-libs. The idea is not to reproduce an exact copy of the original, particularly if it is too vocally demanding. You should, however, aim to vary your phrasing, as this is an indicator of how mature a musician you are.

Music Theatre Singing

Use the same method to learn show music. Obviously the ad-libbing and improvisation elements will not be as relevant. If you play an instrument it can be an advantage, particularly if you are learning the song from the printed sheet music. You may be able to work out the melody. If you don't play or can't read music well, you may know someone who can record it for you.

There are different things to concentrate on depending upon the type of music you are singing. In music theatre the emphasis may be more on character performance. Certainly you need strong delivery of the words (see the *Interpretation* section, page 134). Pay close attention to the dynamics (louds and softs) marked in the music. Employing dynamic contrast can really bring a song to life. Don't feel you have to 'belt' everything out in order to achieve a strong performance – moments of (quiet) tenderness and beauty are equally as powerful.

Classical Singing

Again, you can use the same method to learn classical repertoire. Be careful if you are singing in a foreign language. Make efforts to get your pronunciation accurate. I used to get foreign-language speakers to read the words onto tape for me. I would also back it up by listening to the original wherever possible.

It is essential to have the accompaniment with which to practice. You may have a friend who could play it for you. If not, it will definitely be worth paying a professional accompanist to run through it with you before the audition. Singing with an accompanist or coach is a very different experience to singing at home in your bedroom. They will help you with dynamics and phrasing, and by working together you will become familiar with the accompaniment.

If you are singing choral music, following the score while singing along with a recording of the piece is invaluable.

Artemis Music publishes an excellent product called *Handel's Messiah From Scratch*. There are four different editions (for soprano, alto, tenor and bass) that take all the choruses from the Messiah and highlight the relevant part. They come with 2 CDs: on CD1 there are full orchestral recordings of each chorus with the relevant voice part (e.g. the soprano line in the soprano edition) subtly increased in volume; on CD2 there is a selection of helpful warm-ups and exercises.

Getting Technical

Whatever style of music you are singing, aim to sing well technically. The basic technique is the same and you use your 'ear' to decide what sound you want to make. Remember, you have the choice as a singer.

Here is a checklist of the main areas of technique on which to focus:

- Make sure you have worked out where to breathe.
- Practice the words singing on the vowel.
- Work on where you are resonating the sound.
- Check you are not pushing your chest register too high.
- Try some of the bodywork exercises as you practice, e.g. the pot on the head, arm swinging etc. (see page 39).

Learn your material thoroughly; the better you rehearse it, the better the performance. You usually find that the more you sing a song, the easier it becomes and then you can concentrate on delivery. The following chapter on performance is relevant to any singer in an audition situation or when singing live.

CHAPTER 17 SUMMARY

- The golden rule for any audition is: BE FULLY PREPARED.

- Look your best, but wear clothes in which you can sing comfortably, and that reflect the kind of music for which you are auditioning.

- If the choice of material is yours, choose your songs carefully: generally a slow number and a more up-tempo one – sing your best first.

- Make sure you have a copy of the music for the accompanist in the right key.

- You must know the song inside out – 'over-learn' your material.

- Whichever style of music you are singing, you should aim to sing your piece well technically. Use the checklist above.

Chapter 18
Performance

For many people, performing in public for the first time is a daunting prospect. It can certainly be a nerve-wracking experience, regardless of the occasion. Indeed, even the most seasoned performers suffer from nerves.

But don't worry, I am going to give you some strategies to help you prepare for performing. In this section I talk about general preparation, projection, song delivery and interpretation. I shall then discuss stage fright and give you some exciting, mental visualization techniques that will help you cope with this as well as improve your overall performance.

As far as I'm concerned, live performance is what it's all about. Don't be dispirited if your first efforts are disappointing – singing live gets easier the more you do it. I hope the following will allow you to feel more at ease in your performing. The more relaxed and prepared you are, the more you will enjoy your performance, and the better it is likely to be.

Preparation

As we emphasized in the auditioning section, you need to learn your material well. I know sometimes – despite all your best intentions – you will just not have had enough time to rehearse thoroughly.

Having said that, try to learn your material really well. With the nerves of performance it is easy for things to go wrong.

If you look uncertain and nervous when you sing, then the audience will pick up on this. They will end up feeling ill at ease themselves, which in turn prevents them from being able to relax and enjoy the performance.

If you find learning material difficult, use the methods described in the chapter on *Auditioning* (see page 123). If you are going to sing more than one song, make sure you know your running order.

Projection

When you perform a song you should **project** it to the audience. Projection means 'throwing' or 'casting' out. Many people imagine that you achieve this by pushing the sound out as loudly as possible. However, remember everything I have said about good technique and resonance. You are your instrument. If you push the sound out you will risk losing resonance, support and in all likelihood, after time, your voice. You need to draw the sound into your body to get optimum power and resonance.

Projection is much more than just belting out a song at the top of your voice. It is about putting a song across with feeling and meaning. A performance does not have to be loud for it to be powerful. You want to draw the audience in to you and move them. The more conviction and emotional intensity you have as a performer the better.

Eva Cassidy is a great example of a singer who was able to communicate maximum emotional intensity. Not only did she possess a truly beautiful voice; she also had a rare capacity to engage the audience in a performance that can only be described as spellbinding.

You should project some of your personality to the listener. It is important as a performer to connect with your audience on a personal level. If you ever get the chance to see the lovely Brazilian singer Ive Mendes, take it. Ive has extraordinary individual charm and charisma and is simply mesmerizing on stage. This is largely due to the special way she interacts and communicates with her audience.

People are drawn in consciously and, as a matter of fact, unconsciously by all kinds of things you do with your body. It could be that you maintain strong eye contact with the audience or that, through gesture and expression, you can successfully put across warmth and self-confidence.

Some artists are adept at using hand signals and gestures to communicate; others will capture and hold the attention of their audience by energetically moving around the stage. There is no one approach or personality type that will reach out to an audience and draw them in.

I would, however, recommend that you spend some time closely watching the really big stars. Note what they are doing with their eyes, bodies, hands and arms, especially those things that appear tangibly to bring something out in the audience. Now try building some of these things into your own performance, all the time monitoring their effect and retaining those elements that seem to get the right reaction.

When you are performing, focus is crucially important. If you are unfocused the audience will quickly lose interest in you. They need to believe totally in you as a performer. If you lack focus, you will lack authority. This is a key part of projection.

What you do with your eyes is very important. If you look at the audience, they will respond to you. Eye contact is the most basic form of communication.

However hard they try, some people find this incredibly difficult. If you are one of these people, try focusing on the hairlines of individuals in the audience, or the tops of their heads. This is much better than just staring into space. You will still get the response from the audience you want without having to stare them straight in the eyes.

Whatever size venue you happen to be singing in, remember you need to sing to the people at the back as well as the front. Your performance will only carry as far as you look.

Watching a singer who is just staring out into the distance switches me off as a listener. The unconscious exchange runs something like: if they're not bothered about looking at me, I can't be bothered to listen to them.

Not being able to achieve eye contact with an audience may also suggest a lack of confidence and, again, if you feel the singer is nervy, you will not be relaxed as a listener. Most of us need adrenalin to ensure we give our best performance and facing the audience is part of what gets it flowing. Those artists who communicate strongly with their audience give the most powerful performances.

So, projection involves a number of things, but remember, you don't have to push your voice to unreasonable limits in order to achieve it.

Song Delivery

You need energy, focus, commitment and emotion to put across a song well: take Mick Jagger and Placido Domingo – two very different singers, yet similar in that they both possess these attributes in abundance. Although the style of music they sing is clearly dissimilar, both singers have real charisma and a powerful stage presence, causing you to be drawn into their performance.

Obviously, being on top of your technique when you sing will make the singing a lot more reliable and polished. However, having a perfect technique, many of you will be delighted to hear, is not the be all and end all. Some great artists have not got the best voices but their delivery of a song is very powerful.

Words

Chord structure, melody and instrumentation are obviously the keys to the mood or emotion of any song or piece of music. The lyrics also have an important part to play.

Regardless of the style of music, you have to really mean the words of a song to put them across convincingly (or at least look/sound like you mean them). The listener should be left with a strong impression of the meaning of the song and be moved in some way – left feeling optimistic, happy, sad or thoughtful. If you have an emotional 'thought' when you sing (happy, sad, angry), this will come across in your singing and 'speak' to the listener. It will give your performance an attitude or emotional edge.

Stylistically, in classical and show music, the words are more pronounced than in jazz and rock and pop, and there is greater emphasis on the consonants. D's and t's and other word endings, for example, are generally 'harder' and more deliberate.

In music theatre particularly, the singer's diction needs to be clear, as the form obviously involves the telling of a story or drama. However, in jazz and rock and pop the delivery of the words is traditionally more laid-back and conversational. However you pronounce the words, remember the emphasis should always be on the vowel, to ensure optimum resonance.

If you have a song that requires you to fit a lot of words into a short space, try taking the pressure off the front of your mouth. If you strive to force the words out, your tongue will get stuck and you will trip over them.

Imagine that rather than spitting the words out with your lips, teeth and tongue, you articulate them further back in your mouth. Your tongue should feel springy and light and your lips should just gently touch when they need to. It is almost as if the words are running towards your mouth, jumping in and springing into the back.

Fast rappers are great exponents of this. Check out Messiah Bolical's amazing rap on 'Eenie Meenie' from Craig David's *Slicker Than Your Average* album. The speed of it is mind-blowing, and if you ever have a go, you will realize that fast rapping is almost impossible if placed too 'forward'.

Try saying these tongue twisters firstly articulating at the front of your mouth and then further back.

1. Peter's pity put pretty peaches playing pinball proudly parking partying puppets.

2. Tatty twitchers treated terrible terrifying torches tawdry tricks to tie tattooed turtles.

3. Lately little laughs last longer largely liking littering looting lorry loads of lullabies

4. Rich riders run rings around rollicking rumbling ridiculous rockslides

5. Saving Sally saw Samuel see some sandwiches sailing swiftly south

---

People who have problems pronouncing their 'r's (sounding like 'w's) will need to articulate more with their tongues. The 'w' sound is made by the mouth shape being slightly too round.

American Accent

A great deal of popular music is sung with an American accent. This is because much of it has its roots in the blues. It just doesn't sound authentic if you sing most rock and pop music without some sort of American accent. You can overdo it, of course (don't adopt a fake Texan drawl if you can help it) but, for example, English-sounding 'me's' and 'my's' just sound too straight (too 'Julie Andrews', if you know what I mean). It can take a while to become comfortable with it. Taping your efforts is a good way to check you sound 'authentic' rather than phoney.

Obviously, there will always be successful singers and bands that have a definite regional sound – I'm all for it.

Sophie Ellis Bextor is an excellent example of someone who doesn't sing with an American accent. While working with Sophie I asked about her pronunciation. She told me that several years ago she used to sing with the band Theaudience. During one rehearsal she spontaneously changed a word (I can't remember exactly what it was – let's say it was 'can't') from the American pronunciation to 'Southern' English. She liked the sound of it and decided from then on to sing with this accent. It has since become her hallmark. Listen how she sings 'dance' in her big hit 'Murder on the Dancefloor'.

Interpretation

I am sure you have heard the phrase 'making a song your own' – well, this is what interpretation is all about. It means taking a song and putting your own personal mark on it. There are many things to consider when working on interpretation: technique, words, phrasing, improvisation, emotion, intensity, sensitivity, energy and focus. I have given you a lot of information about all of these, so it is up to you to put it into practice.

It may be that you are singing a classical aria that demands beautiful line and tone, or a song from a show that requires plenty of character. You may be singing an improvisatory jazz piece or a sustained or up-tempo rock and pop song. All of these demand different skills and qualities, or, I could say, a combination of many similar things.

1. Try singing your song with an emotional 'thought' – think happy, sad, angry, vulnerable, and see what difference it makes.

2. Practice emphasizing the meaning of the words.

3. Work on your phrasing: singing behind the beat, on it, ahead of the beat.

4. Try to improvise around the melody. Don't be overambitious. Small excursions from the tune are fine for starters.

The Band Vocalist

Everything I have said about performance is relevant whether you are a soloist or a band member. If you are gigging there are, however, some other considerations.

There is no doubt that stepping out on to a stage for the first time in front of an audience – however well-rehearsed you are – can be a terrifying ordeal. It is true to say that the more you do it, the easier it gets, but there are a number of things you can work on to help you prepare yourself better and build your confidence.

Firstly, learn your material thoroughly. Make sure that all your songs are really well 'sung in'. Generally speaking, the more you have sung a song, the easier it becomes and the less likely you are to strain your voice.

It is a good idea to 'over-learn' your songs. When you are on stage and actually facing the audience you may freeze. The words are usually the first thing to go and that can feel very scary, so you want them to be almost second nature. The more familiar you are with your material the better. You will be able to relax more easily and this will make you feel freer to improvise.

If you are doing a gig or showcase make sure you know your running order – there is nothing worse than an embarrassing pause while everyone gets their act together.

Learning to perform on stage takes practice. Obviously, some people are naturals and feel totally at home, but most of us have to work at it. Initially, moving around the stage can feel awkward. If you feel you are a natural 'mover' then great, but if you look uncomfortable, the audience will share your discomfort. Holding a microphone helps, as you then have something to do with your hands. Some singers feel more comfortable using a mic stand as it literally gives them something more to hold on to. Percussion instruments, like a tambourine or cow bell, can also be useful props.

The instrumental breaks can be tricky. You need to keep your focus here. If you are not the kind of singer who enjoys leaping around, you, above all, need to look like you are well into the music. Look at the audience, and keep eye contact (I think this is the most powerful technique). It can work well just standing still, foot-tapping. Some singers prefer to look down, others even turn round with their backs to the audience. It is down to you and what you are comfortable with. Whatever you do, you must carry it out with conviction, but make sure you have practiced it first. Don't leave it until your first gig to try something out.

It can be easier being on stage if you have an instrument to hide behind, but this doesn't mean that your performance can be lazy. As I mentioned earlier, the instrumentalist has to consider how they use their bodies so that there is no cost to the singing.

One of the things that frightens so many people, often more than the singing itself, is interacting with the audience at the start of a gig and in between numbers. Many avoid doing any work on it, simply because they feel too embarrassed or self-conscious.

If it is your job (and invariably, if you are the lead vocalist, it will be) to provide links, script them; rehearse your comments or jokes so you can deliver them confidently. Many singers don't say much at all, which can be fine, but don't rely on being able to come up with something brilliant on the spot. Interacting with the audience can be a vital part of your performance.

Watch people who are good at it and analyze what they are doing. A lot of what sounds spontaneous will, in fact, be rehearsed – you will know this if you have seen certain shows more than once. Try not to be too ambitious; keep it fairly simple initially. In time working with the audience will come more naturally.

Try not to get too carried away in the excitement of performance. I have heard of guitarists getting cut fingers and tambourine players bruising their thighs! More seriously though, if you lose your focus you could end up pushing your voice too far and doing some damage. This could range from a small swelling of the cords to, if repeated regularly, the formation of nodules.

Guard against forcing your voice while gigging: always remember to warm up – either by using exercises or, at least, some gentle singing. Everybody is different and some voices warm up more slowly than others, but try to do about ten minutes. Don't do too much and tire out your voice before you have started (avoid overdoing it in the soundcheck). Don't start 'cold' – you won't sound as good, and you stand more chance of harming your voice. I shall be going through warm-ups in more detail later (see page 169).

If you can't hear yourself on stage, don't push it: there is no point. The chances are that no one else will be able to hear you either – even if you are screaming at the top of your voice. Unfortunately, not all sound systems are very good. With any luck your monitors will be loud enough, but quite often you will feel you are fighting a losing battle.

Trying to get the band to turn it down a notch is usually pretty difficult. Stand your ground; even turning down a bit can really help you. Make them see that if the band loses its singer due to voice problems, they are history!

Some people find that earplugs help. For those with more cash, 'inner ears' are very useful. You will have seen singers on TV wearing these discreet earphones, molded to the shape of their ears. They allow you to hear your own voice properly, along with a mix of the track, or band, making it easier to avoid forcing your voice against the track, and hopefully help with pitching. Inner ears take a while to get used to, so if you are using them make sure you have rehearsed well with them before singing live. Some singers have themselves turned up so loud that they sing way out of tune!

Gigging Sound

Those of us who have done a lot of gigs will have experienced the horrors of terrible sound equipment, and sometimes equally terrible sound engineers. If you end up struggling to overcome some kind of giant acoustic octopus while you are trying to sing, it can certainly take away the pleasure. If you have a good sound balance on stage it makes a massive difference. Here is some information about equipment and on-stage sound, as well as a few tips to get things running smoothly.

Monitor speakers allow each person on stage to have their own personal mix. For example, the singer might have very loud vocals, including a good blend of backing vocals, a bit of guitar, a fair amount of keyboards – as they have no acoustic level – plus a small amount of bass.

There are also side-fill speakers that are designed to give a complete mix of the on-stage sound to suit the band. These speakers are very important because they allow you to move away from your monitor and have more freedom on stage.

Always try to strike up a rapport with the person in charge of the sound. You will probably not be able to hear yourself as well as the rest of the band. A few friendly words early on will encourage the sound person to be more attentive to your changing needs during the gig. If you don't hit it off, it can be a nightmare.

All vocalists want to be heard above the band (and I would heartily agree with that), but appreciate that it is difficult to get the drums below a certain level. Yes, I know, they're always too loud.

Drummer Joke No. 67
Producer to drummer: 'Can we try that again but this time with more dynamics.'
Drummer: 'Okay, I'll try, but I'm playing as loud as I can!'

Drummer Joke No. 88
Q: What is the difference between a drummer and a drum machine?
A: You only have to punch the rhythm into a drum machine once.

Drummer Joke No. 99
Q: What do you call a guy who hangs around with musicians?
A: A drummer.

To avoid giving you the impression that I have it in for drummers exclusively, I would add that it will also help if you don't have the guitar stack pointing directly at your ear.

Singers invariably have no reverb in their monitors as reverb goes back into the mic and makes the sound muddy. So don't give the monitor engineer a hard time if you were expecting it.

Stage Fright

Relaxation is a powerful tool to combat stage fright. As I have mentioned previously, breathing exercises have a calming effect. They can help stop your breathing and your body from going into panic mode.

Giving yourself time to lie on the floor and focus on your breath (see *Breathing Exercises,* page 17) will help you to overcome any feelings of panic. Pre-show nerves are not necessarily a bad thing, as most of us need a certain amount of adrenalin to pull off a good performance.

By the way, if you suffer badly from nerves then I have to tell you alcohol is not the answer. Many people think that a quick drink before they go on will steady them. While alcohol may well make you feel a bit more relaxed, the downside is that your vocals can suffer. Alcohol increases the blood supply to your vocal cords, causing them to swell. As a result, the sound you produce will not be as reliable as usual.

One singer I worked with studied method acting to help her deal with stage fright. She was able to switch off from her fear and visualize herself in non-threatening situations – scrubbing her back in the bath or lying on a beach. It worked very well for her, particularly in slow numbers, but it wouldn't work for everyone – there is a danger of drifting off and losing connection with your audience.

Visualization

As we have already seen, mental imagery is used a great deal when singing. Sometimes, simply by visualizing something – like when we direct the sound into different resonating places – it will happen. Visualization techniques can also be used to give you a more positive attitude towards your performance.

To give the best vocal performance you need to be practically, physically and mentally prepared. Many performers like to have a quiet period before going on stage to relax, get rid of nerves and focus their mind and energy.

Many use some form of **positive imaging** (like that used by top sportsmen and women) to get themselves into the optimum frame of mind before performing. Finding the right environment in which to do this can often prove difficult, especially given cramped venues, but it is definitely worth trying.

There are many different 'positive visualization' techniques, but here is a simple and effective one to try.

Find a quiet place, close your eyes and relax. Listen, calmly, to your breathing. Concentrate on breathing out (this is the relaxing part of breathing).

Visualize yourself singing a particular song from start to finish really well – your best possible performance. You could use a memory of a particular occasion, but it doesn't have to be. Focus your mind on what you look like and what you are doing with your body.

Next, using the same image or 'film' of yourself, listen to how you sound when you are singing really well. Go through the whole song again.

Now go through it once more, concentrating on what it feels like when you are singing really well. Focus on what it feels like emotionally as well as physically, or technically.

The important thing is to go over the song three times, focusing, in turn, on the visual, auditory and kinaesthetic (feeling) modes. Don't miss one out – the technique is just not as powerful if you do.

What you are creating here is known as a *rehearsed positive state*. It is an exceptionally powerful tool and can make a big difference to how you think of yourself as a performer and consequently how well you are able to perform. It is an empowering technique that deeply reinforces the feeling and belief that you can sing really well. When you perform for real you can draw on these positive thoughts and feelings, enabling you to maximize your performance.

In order to help with this process, you can employ what are known as *mental anchors*. As you mentally rehearse the song, for example, you can associate the feelings and thoughts arising from successfully navigating a particularly difficult part of your vocal with the touching of a specific part of your body. Then when you come to sing, just by touching that body part the same positive visualization is triggered.

For example, while you are positively visualizing how you are sounding at a certain point in the song, you can touch the top of your left thigh with the fingers of your left hand. When you are singing, you touch yourself in the same place and that 'memory' or positive state is triggered.

Visualization can be extremely useful before any performance, but you can build it into your general practice.

A Cappella Performance

Often in auditions you have to sing without any accompaniment, but it is not just for auditions that you may have to sing unaccompanied, or *a cappella*. There is a real history to unaccompanied singing. There are many groups that include *a cappella* songs in their sets or, indeed only sing unaccompanied – take, for example, barbershop quartets.

I love singing in harmony: there is nothing quite like it. I used to sing in a close-harmony jazz group. It was purely for fun but we sang wonderful arrangements penned by the inspirational jazz pianist and teacher Pete Churchill. Thanks Pete. His love of music and enthusiasm are infectious. I learned so much about singing together as a group, phrasing, dynamics and improvisation in these sessions. What I learned has stayed with me and much of it I use day in, day out.

Singing together well is a real discipline. The absolute masters are Take Six. If you haven't heard them you should treat yourself. They are all highly trained musicians and they use their voices as instruments. Indeed, they provide their own 'instrumental' backing with their voices. Their arrangements and harmonies are so inventive and they sing together as an incredibly tight unit. The balance of their voices is perfect and their phrasing remarkable. One of my favorite tracks is 'Get Away Jordan' from the album *Take Six*.

I have worked with a number of pop bands over the years, helping them to prepare *a cappella* 'snippets' for TV and radio appearances. This is always popular – the main idea, I guess, being that it shows they really can sing! Usually they will do an arrangement of a small part of their latest single, or one of their hits, maybe only singing the chorus. They generally keep it short and sweet, although sometimes they may want something more adventurous.

I have a specific approach when working with a group. Firstly, I make sure everyone knows their line, or harmony. Then we work on these until everyone is singing them well. We then move on to group dynamics – getting the louds and softs in the same place. Then I concentrate on phrasing, making sure they are all singing the same length phrases with the same emphasis. Next, I focus attention on the words and vowel sounds.

The beginnings and ends of phrases need to be tight otherwise the singing will sound sloppy. Ragged 't's and 'd's sound awful. If endings are proving tricky, I give one of the singers the responsibility for sounding them (with the others just 'ghosting').

Getting them to listen closely to each other is vital. They must not just grimly hold on to their line and shut out everyone else. Learning to hear their line as part of the whole is crucial, otherwise the tuning and phrasing will never be good enough. Looking at each other while rehearsing works well (until, as often happens, they all start laughing).

I usually appoint one band member as MD (musical director). Sometimes this doesn't go down too well. You have to be aware of egos and to some, it looks like favoritism (fame affects some people in funny ways, you know – but my lips are sealed!).

The MD will be responsible for giving starting notes, counting in and generally keeping the whole thing together. They can do this by using a combination of eye contact, gentle conducting, or a slight head gesture. (Unfortunately, they run the risk of getting an unwelcome gesture back from those not chosen to be MD!)

CHAPTER 18 SUMMARY

- When singing live, you need to learn to project or, in other words, put a song across with feeling and meaning.

- The audience is drawn in at an unconscious level by all kinds of things you do with your body.

- It is particularly important to achieve eye contact with your audience.

- Regardless of the style of music, you have to really *mean* the words of a song to put them across convincingly.

- A singer's diction needs to be clearer in opera or show music than it does in jazz or rock and pop, chiefly because these forms involve the telling of a story or drama.

- It is much easier to sing very wordy songs and fast raps if you articulate further back in your mouth.

- Generally speaking, most rock and pop and R&B singing only sounds authentic if sung in an American accent, although there are several notable 'English' regional exceptions.

- Interpretation involves taking a song and putting your own personal mark on it.

- There are many things to consider when working on interpretation: technique, words, phrasing, improvisation, emotion, intensity, sensitivity, energy, focus, etc.

- Band vocalists should always rehearse fully, be clear about running orders, practice their stagecraft and links, strike up a rapport with the sound engineer, warm up properly and look after their voices.

- Breathing exercises and visualization techniques can help to relax and prepare a singer before a performance.

- A systematic approach to group harmony singing is suggested in this chapter.

Chapter 19
Recording And Studio Work

Singing in a studio is a very different experience to singing live. Recording vocals well is something I feel passionate about. The singing on many recordings is, to my ears, nowhere near as good as it could be. From a professional point of view I find this very frustrating. There are many producers who get great vocals out of their artists, but there are many more who don't. One of my specialist areas is working in studios with singers, helping them to record their tracks – something I really love doing.

Recording Vocals

There are many different ways of going about recording vocals. Obviously much of it is determined by the equipment and resources you have available to you.

What I like to hear in a good vocal are: good tuning, great phrasing and feel, emotion, character, energy, and a great tone. In other words, all the elements that combine to make a great live performance.

Some singers prefer to sing the whole song all the way through; others prefer to record it in sections. My personal preference is a mixture of the two. I like to start with the singer running the song a couple of times to get a good 'vibe' going. Then I like to break it up into sections: record the first verse and bridge, then the second verse and bridge. Sometimes I will just do the verses, then the bridges. It really depends on how vocally demanding the song is. Then I may do the middle eight, followed by the choruses, harmonies and ad-libs.

Often the chorus will be higher than the rest of the song. Consequently, if you do a number of takes it can become tiring quite quickly. This is why I recommend that you get the bulk of the singing done first.

Nothing, however, is set in stone. Some singers prefer to record the song 'live' as they find they get a better feel. They will do several takes all the way through and choose the best one. Many singers find it difficult to make a song consistently good all the way through. Even if you record in sections, you may find that you will go back and rework the beginning. The more you work on a song, the more ideas you get.

Most producers 'track' vocals, which means that the singer repeats exactly what they have sung over again. These two 'tracks' will then be played simultaneously. It thickens up the vocal sound. On backing vocals and harmonies especially, three or more 'tracks' are sometimes added.

Often, to add depth to the sound, the lead line is added (quietly) an octave lower. Whispers are also used to add texture. This is where the singer delivers the words in time with the track, but in a whispered sound.

There are some things that are simply not achievable in a studio. I once witnessed a guy masquerading as a producer who wanted to create a 'live vibe', so he suggested that the singer hand-hold the mic. In a professional studio this is a 'no go', as the mics are so sensitive they pick up the slightest noise. The level is carefully set and if you move the mic around the volume would jump up and down like a yo-yo.

For a final word on the recording of vocals I turn to my long-time friend and Grammy-winning producer, Kipper.

> 'I have had the good fortune to produce some of my favorite singers of all time. James Taylor, Mary J Blige, Shawn Colvin and, of course Sting, to name four!! Singers of this calibre I believe are born and not bred, however, they too need to employ focus, discipline and technique in order to maximize their potential.
>
> As a producer my role is to get a great sound for the performer to work with, create a suitable atmosphere and ambience that is relaxed and conducive to the song, and to be a positive sounding board able to offer ideas or advice when needed.
>
> I always like to have the singer in the control room with me when recording lead vocals. This enables me to have a more intense working relationship with the artist and the song, whilst removing the clinical "studio" vibe that a vocal booth and glass wall can create.

Some handy tips:

Record and keep absolutely everything you sing or play; one never knows when an inspirational moment may arrive.

If you are having tuning problems, remove one side of the headphones to reference your voice through the air. You may find there is too much reverb on your voice or that your vocal balance is wrong.

Never feel that "this is the one". Each take is work in progress and all the details you may obsess over today may have evaporated tomorrow. Simply enjoy the song and be in the moment.'

Looking After Yourself In The Vocal Booth

You need to look after your voice when you are recording. Make sure you warm up properly beforehand – not too much, though, as you will probably have a lot of singing to do. Drink lots of water and take rests when you feel you need to. Don't let the producer bully you by making you sing if your voice feels really tired – you risk damaging it. Don't let people smoke around you.

Some producers have a real flair for recording vocals and getting the best out of a singer. Unfortunately, there are others who, when it comes to working with singers, don't know what they are doing. Some may have done a bit of singing themselves, or had the odd singing lesson. I find it irritating, though, when they try to make out they are an authority on singing when patently they are not. These people can often confuse a singer (a little bit of knowledge being a dangerous thing) by trying to push them to do something technically inappropriate.

We are all different and, in the case of singing, it is most definitely not true that 'one size fits all'. What works for one singer may well not work for another. Many producers will try to push a singer to their limit by demanding that they sing material much too high for their voice, or by expecting them to keep going even when their voice is showing clear signs of fatigue and strain. They may, as I mentioned, insist that the singer tries something alien and technically inappropriate or unhelpful.

It is true that you need to make yourself work hard, and that time in the studio is very expensive, but that doesn't mean you have to strain your voice and risk temporary or permanent damage. If someone asks you to do something that is continually vocally uncomfortable, there is a case for standing up for yourself and simply refusing to do it.

Note: never use any vocal sprays or chemical remedies to get you through a vocal. If your voice has packed up there is a good reason for it. Using these things in order to continue singing is akin to applying a painkilling spray to an athlete's torn or damaged muscle and expecting them to carry on competing – not recommended!

Backing Vocals And Harmonies

Many songs do not sound complete without the addition of backing vocals. Good BVs enhance and often totally transform a song by adding depth, color and excitement. On recordings, the solo artist will often sing their own BVs or they will be sung by professional backing/session singers. In a live situation other band members might be called upon to do a few.

Backing singing is an art in itself. The top session singers have all got very good voices and are generally excellent performers. They really know their stuff and have worked hard at it over the years. They will have listened to a great amount and variety of music, paying particular attention to style and phrasing and will have copied and practiced the best examples.

However, not everyone needs to be an amazing singer to do BVs. Many instrumentalists in bands have to sing them, and indeed it is an asset for a musician to be able to sing strong BVs – there is no doubt that you are a more attractive proposition to bands and agencies if you can. Interestingly, a lot of instrumentalists come to me for help with their backing singing. Some end up discovering voices they never thought they had, and even move on to singing lead vocals.

Backing vocals can be used in many different ways. On recorded tracks there would usually be more BVs than live. However, if someone is singing along to a backing track, most of the BVs will be on it (often the lead is also there, but just reduced in volume a bit). When singing live with a band, pre-recorded BV tracks are sometimes used and would be triggered by one of the instrumentalists.

Backing vocals are often used to enhance a lead line – tracking it, as I have already mentioned, or singing it an octave higher or lower. Harmonizing the lead in 2, 3 or 4 parts is common. You wouldn't want to do it all the way through a song, but in the right places it can sound great. Sometimes just harmonizing the last one or two words of a phrase can be very effective.

Some people have a natural ability to be able to pick out a harmony line effortlessly. Most singers have the capability but it just takes practice. BVs can be simple or complex, depending on the music, but here are a few suggestions that will give you a starting point for developing your BVs.

If you are singing in two parts, the easiest harmony line to take is a 3rd above the lead line. So, for example, if the melody started on a C you would start on the E above, You would then move in exactly the same way as the lead.

Another simple line would be a 6th below. That would mean that if the lead were on a C you would start on the E below and then move with the melody.

When singing a three-part harmony, base it around a triad (the first, third and fifth notes of the chord you are playing). Don't always sing this in its root position; you can invert it (turn it around): for example, you could have the 3rd at the bottom, then the 5th and then the root (or 1st note of the scale) on top.

You won't always be moving with the melody, or singing the words. Backing vocals can be used more as a textural filler and often are structured around instrumental ideas found in a song – maybe a guitar or keyboard riff. These would usually be sung on ooh's, ah's and hums, but still they follow the same harmonic patterns. I love scrunchy harmonies and, obviously, there are many other more complicated ones you can use, but I'm trying to keep it pretty straightforward. All the harmonies I have mentioned are based around the movement of the chords.

Don't overdo the BVs and make things sound too cluttered. Usually the lead singer will sing at least one verse on their own. The backing may then come in for the second verse, or the chorus. In a chorus you may want to emphasize certain words, making the backing more chant-like. It may answer the lead line. In some songs the backing takes over and forms the 'hook' of a song and the lead singer is then free to improvise over the top. Many songs end in this way.

Some people find sticking to a harmony line difficult. It just takes practice. There are a few things you can try that might help. First start by listening to songs and try picking out the backing and joining in. Next, take a simple tune. Tape yourself singing it and then try to work out a simple harmony – maybe a 3rd above – and keep singing along with yourself. The more confident you get, the more ambitious you will become.

How you sing the backing vocals is also very important. It is no good if you have all the theory but consistently sing out of tune or very weakly. You need to work on your technique. It is important for you to be confident with your own singing and to know how to avoid 'pushing' your voice too hard.

Instrumentalists who have reasonably high voices often complain to me that they are forever being asked to take the high harmony. They find this is all right in the studio, but once they are gigging their voices are shot after a couple of numbers. My best tip is to sing in *falsetto* or *head voice* for men or *head voice* or *mixed register* for women. Many people are reluctant to try this at first, but when they do, they soon discover how it protects their voice and, with practice, how they can get it to sound strong. (Remember, always 'think down' as you go up!)

Make sure that BVs are well rehearsed. It makes such a difference if they are tight. Ensure you have all decided exactly where you are beginning and ending notes, where you are getting louder or softer, and what vowel sounds you are using. Make sure no individual's voice is sticking out: it is important for the sound to be a reasonable blend. Practice without any accompaniment so that you can really hear each other. It is surprising how many people have never thought of doing this.

Whether preparing BVs for live gigs or recordings, they are well worth spending time on since they can make all the difference to a song.

Mic Technique

People often imagine there is some great secret to mastering the use of a mic. And it amuses me to see singing coaches giving such prominence to the learning of 'mic technique' in their promotional material. In fact, there is very little to learn, and using a mic properly is something that you can master very quickly.

Most importantly, you need to know how to produce an even sound, so if you are singing high or low, the volume should be consistent. This is achieved by moving into the mic for softer or lower notes and away from the mic for louder or higher notes. If you are using a hand-held mic, you move the mic itself. Don't overdo this. Some people develop a habit of pulling the mic away much too far and then the sound disappears altogether or comes and goes in waves.

Hold the mic in front of your mouth, not so close that your lips are touching it, but near enough for the sound to be picked up.

You need to mind your 'p's and 'd's because they can 'pop' on the mic. Also, in order to avoid sibilance (hissing 's' sounds), rather than singing directly into it on some phrases, you should move *across* the mic. As is the case with all aspects of mic technique, this will become second nature with practice.

Most singers like to have reverb added to the sound. Reverb electronically creates an ambience for the dry signal. It can be set to give the impression of singing anywhere from a small bathroom to a huge hall. It is much harder singing with a dry sound.

If you have tried singing in a small or cluttered room, and then in a church or big empty hall, you will know the difference. The sound is absorbed by furniture, curtains etc. In a large hall or even an empty room it is free to ring around and resonate. Singing automatically feels easier. If you haven't experienced this before, next time you clear a room for decorating, have a good sing!

A word of warning. It is not good practice only to sing with a mic. You will never establish a good technique this way. It will prevent you from developing support, resonance, sustain and evenness of tone amongst other things.

Someone came to me after being taught by a well-known teacher of rock and pop singers. In her lessons she had only ever sung songs using a mic. Having had lessons for three years with this person, she had developed no awareness of resonance, openness, body use, support or breath control. I find this totally unbelievable: sure, it's a good idea to rehearse with a mic if you are going to perform, but not all the time. My advice to you if this happens in your singing lessons is don't go!

Lip-Synching

Some singers, when miming, hold the mic really close to their mouths to cover up poor lip-synching. Certainly, lip-synching can be tricky to get tight if you have a lot of words or a rap to deliver. For lip-synching to look good you have to work at it. Practice by watching yourself in a mirror along with the track. Actually singing the song will help to make your lip-synching accurate and convincing.

People do put an importance on good lip-synching. I have actually been employed to work on some films and videos to ensure that the lip-synching looks authentic.

Sight Singing

Sight singing is the ability to sing music from a printed score without having previously rehearsed it. You do not need to read music or sight sing to be a great singer – many professional singers do neither and will never need to learn. However, being able to read music has many advantages, and having the ability to sight-sing can make life a lot easier. In addition, it will mean that you are more desirable for certain singing jobs.

In order to sight-sing, you first need to be able to read music. Clearly, reading music is not something you pick up overnight and it definitely takes practice. Those who have played an instrument from an early age normally have an advantage since they will usually have studied written music. If you are going to sing in a choir or have ambitions to be a session singer, there are obvious advantages to sharpening up your reading.

Classical musicians tend to be the best readers as they will generally have studied written music for many years, depending on how long they have been playing. A great number of musicians, particularly in the rock and pop field, don't read a note of music. This is true of many of the best instrumentalists and vocalists I have known. These people have incredibly well developed 'ears' and have never had to read a note. A lot of them, however, share a common (often secret) desire to be able to read. For many, it feels a bit like trying to join a club to which they don't really belong.

Understandably, if you play brilliantly by ear already, it might seem pointless to start learning notation from scratch. 'Is it worth it?', I hear you ask.

Well, learning to read music has many advantages. If you are singing with a choir and following scores it is obviously a huge help. You will be able to work out songs from songbooks. If you write your own songs, you can jot down the chords and melody so that you don't lose your ideas.

You can also keep a record of harmonies. I find this incredibly useful with some of the bands I work with, as they quite often have a problem remembering exactly who did what – at least that way I have proof and can help to prevent some of the arguments!

Guitarist Joke No. 44
Q: How do you shut up a guitarist?
A: Put a piece of sheet music in front of him.

Obviously, if you have recording facilities, then you wouldn't have to do this, but often ideas come to you at the least appropriate moments. The way you write them down doesn't have to be 100 per cent accurate. It can be as rough as you like – just a sketch of your ideas. Even if you are only vaguely following the ups and downs of the tune, that may be enough for your purposes.

For those musicians aspiring to professional status, the more skilled you are the better. As a professional singer, you limit your options of work if you can't read. Certainly, much studio work is done by ear, but often there will be a score to read. Turning up for a session and finding a score on the music stand can be a wobbly moment for a non-reader.

Musical notation is really very logical and, although it does take time to learn to read, it is really not all that difficult. There are many books around on music theory and sight singing which are written in user-friendly language. I will limit myself here to a few useful tips.

In order to sight-sing, you need to become familiar with and be able to sing the intervals on the stave – or, in other words, combine what you see on the page with what you hear in your head. An interval is the distance from one note to the next. The interval between A and C, for example, is a third (ABC): between A and E is a fifth (ABCDE): Between A and G is a seventh (ABCDEFG), and so on.

Something that has helped a lot of people to cement the intervals in their head is to link them to a song they know well. Let me explain. You can use the first two notes of a familiar song as an anchor. For example, the song 'Yesterday' starts with a major second; 'Summertime' starts with a major third; 'Auld Lang Syne' is a fourth; 'Scarborough Fair' is a (perfect) fifth; 'My Way' is a major 6th; 'Somewhere' from *West Side Story* is a 7th; 'Over the Rainbow' is an octave. You need to learn to combine what these intervals look like on the stave with what they sound like – so that the pattern is instantly recognizable.

When reading music always think in terms of patterns and shapes, especially when you are looking at a piece for the first time. You need to learn the notes both visually as well as aurally.

It is difficult to learn to read if you don't play an instrument as you will have nothing to use as a point of reference. For this reason, if you are serious about learning to sight-read, I would recommend you buy yourself a keyboard.

You also need to practice reading rhythm and, again, there are many good tutor books around. Work at tapping simple rhythms, gradually increasing their difficulty. You can also use songbooks or scores alongside the appropriate recording. Study the music and follow it while listening to the track. There are books available that have all the band parts transcribed. These are brilliant to work with, as you can follow each part in turn.

Following recordings of choral works, symphonies and concertos is ideal. Start with the simpler works of Classical composers such as Mozart, Haydn and Beethoven – they shouldn't be too hard to follow. If you try a tricky contemporary piece you could put yourself off for life!

CHAPTER 19 SUMMARY

- When recording vocals you should try to achieve good tuning, great phrasing and feel, emotion, character, energy and a great tone.

- Most producers 'track' vocals which means that the singer repeats exactly what they have sung over again in order to thicken up the vocal sound.

- To add depth and texture to the sound, the words are often whispered in time with the lead line, or the melody is sung an octave lower.

- It is important for singers to look after themselves in the vocal booth, by warming up properly and applying good basic voice care.

- Backing singing is an art in itself, but there are some general approaches and skills that you can learn.

- Mic technique is not difficult to learn. It will come easily with experience.

- Most singers do not know how to sight-sing, but if you can, it is a very useful tool to have. It might also make you more desirable for certain singing jobs.

SECTION FIVE:
MAINTENANCE, BREAKDOWN AND RECOVERY

We use our voices continually – at work, at home, in the pub or bar, talking on the phone and, of course, when we sing. Normally our voices work well and rarely let us down. Occasionally some of us do encounter voice problems, and these are invariably connected to the sorts of things we put our voices through.

Professional voice-users are especially prone to breakdown simply because they use their voices more than others do. These people in particular will benefit from observing some basic rules of voice care.

Taking on board what I say in this section may well save you a lot of trouble and, for some, help you to avoid developing long-term voice problems.

Chapter 20
Voice Care

Dos And Don'ts

If you sing regularly it is very important to take good care of your voice. Voice care applies just as much to your speaking voice as it does to your singing voice.

Many of the problems encountered by singers derive from the social environment surrounding their singing performances. Speaking or, more accurately, shouting over loud music is a real strain for most people. Many singers will have sung for a few hours with no problems and then moved on to a noisy club or bar where they have wrecked their voices.

I bought Craig David a large hand-held electronic memory-and-reaction-time game primarily to act as an anchor or reminder not to talk too much before and after gigs. I am pleased to say it served its purpose. Furthermore, since the particular game requires great mental agility and quick reactions, it came as no surprise that he soon became annoyingly brilliant at the thing!

> *Top tip: When speaking over loud music, make your voice as nasal as possible. This will help to prevent you from pushing your voice too much. I have tried it and it works a treat. It is kind of a weird thing to do, admittedly, but I haven't lost any friends as a result yet. Perhaps they have noticed, but are just too polite to tell me, that after a few drinks, I always seem to start sounding like an alien.*

I am not going to pull any punches here. If you are a singer DO NOT SMOKE. I know that many singers do smoke, but aside from negatively affecting your breath control, smoking acts as an irritant. Smoking will make you more prone to sore throats and coughs. When you cough, your vocal cords collide in a brutal fashion. Be warned. It is often when people have bad coughs and carry on singing that serious vocal problems can arise.

It therefore follows that you should try to avoid smoky atmospheres. I suffer terribly if I have been in a smoky environment for any length of time. My voice will always feel rough the next day.

One of the best pieces of advice I can give you is to drink lots of water – not alcohol. I know it sounds boring and not very rock'n'roll, but alcohol, as I have mentioned before, increases the blood supply to your cords and makes them slightly swollen. If they become swollen, this increases the risk of damage. You may feel a bit less nervy after a few drinks but the effect of alcohol on your cords will result in your voice being less reliable than usual. Save the drinks until after the show. Having said that, I wouldn't personally drink alcohol if I had a big show the following day.

Fruit juices can often be too acidic for the voice. A surprising number of people are severely affected by acid reflux; they have to avoid things such as fruit juices and tomatoes otherwise their throats become very sore and their vocal cords swollen. Spicy food is another contributor – sad but true, you curry fans! If you do suffer from this, try to eat at least two hours before you go to bed.

Dairy produce is to be avoided. It creates excess mucus and clogs you up. So, sadly, no milkshakes or chocolate bars before you sing. Some people find bananas 'clagging' as well.

Tea and coffee are not great to drink if you are singing because of their dehydrating effect. Herbal teas and warm water are good.

Avoid ice in your drinks; it will make your cords contract. Honey and lemon are fine, but the mixture won't repair the damage if you have strained your voice. The honey will feel soothing on your throat, the vitamin C in the lemon is good for you, and the water will keep you hydrated, but it will not touch your vocal cords. STEAM is the only real answer.

A steam inhaler can be a godsend for many. You can get these in regular chemists/drugstores. The old-fashioned bowl of hot water and towel over the head version is just as good. When you inhale steam the moisture gets right down to your cords and is very soothing. Many singers use steam rooms for the same reason. I would recommend steaming two to three times a day if you have voice problems.

Rest. It seems obvious, but if your voice is tired or if you have developed problems, the more you can rest your voice the better. When I say rest, I mean from talking as well as singing. Try not to talk on the phone excessively and avoid going any place where you have to raise your voice. Football games are out!

Regular exercise, eating healthily and keeping fit are all important. Remember, you *are* your instrument and the more you take care of it the better. Any sort of aerobic exercise is good. If you are working out in the gym, however, be careful if you are doing a lot of weights or sit-ups; it is easy to strain your voice and get tight around your throat area.

Always warm up before you sing. Five minutes can be sufficient (I shall be dealing with this in detail in the next chapter).

Practice regularly. You will strengthen your voice and increase your awareness of how you are using it.

DO

- Always warm up before singing.

- Drink water (un-iced) and herbal teas.

- Practice regularly.

- Look after your voice in rehearsals.

- If you speak over loud music, make your voice nasal.

- Rest your voice if it is tired or if you have a cold.

- Inhale steam if your voice is tired, you have had a cold, or have been in a smoky environment.

- Keep fit and healthy. Get as much sleep as possible.

DON'T

- Start a rehearsal or a performance cold.

- Drink alcohol before singing.

- Eat fruit juices and iced drinks.

- Eat dairy products, tomatoes, and spicy foods.

- Over-practice.

- Get carried away in rehearsals or sound checks. (Don't sing at full volume all the time.)

- Speak/shout over loud music or shout after performances.

- Cough or clear your throat too vigorously.

- Smoke. Avoid smoky environments.

- Put any strain on the larynx when working out in the gym.

Public Speaking

As well as being a singing coach I also do general voice work with TV presenters and other professional voice users. I work with them to get the best out of their voices and my approach is virtually the same as the one I use with singers.

The emphasis is still on the use of the breath, support, resonance, openness, and having a free body. It is important to make sure that their voices are working efficiently and to iron out any problem areas.

For example, if they are not using the breath properly, their voices will be 'shallow' and may sound 'caught' in their throats – clearly not what you want from a presenter or newsreader. We work on removing any hard edges from their voices.

This does not mean getting rid of character, as that is, of course, important, but sometimes it needs to be toned down a bit, depending on the content of the piece they are delivering.

Schoolteachers are heavy voice users and many suffer from voice problems. While, hopefully, few teachers these days regularly shout at their pupils, the constant use of their voices, particularly when 'projecting' in front of a class, will soon reveal weaknesses and frailties.

People in various other professions are often required to give talks and presentations that can be vocally demanding. In these contexts, there are certain techniques that can be applied which will maximize delivery and help to avoid potential voice problems.

Presentations

Many of the things I say about singing in this book have a direct relevance to normal speech. If you have a presentation or a speech to give, you can practice it using some of the techniques I have already described.

Many people experience a terrible feeling of dread and panic at the thought of making a presentation. If you are one of these, start by using breathing exercises to calm yourself – they will also help you to focus.

As I have already stressed, preparation is the key to good delivery. If you practice the following it will not only vastly improve your confidence but also your delivery.

1.   *Firstly, focus on your breath. Work out where to breathe – you could pencil in breath marks in your text. Rehearse with your hands on your tummy, taking your time and making sure your breath is relaxed, low and not snatched.*

2.   *Practice a section, emphasizing the vowels. Write it out just like the 'nonsense' writing on page 81. Feel the different places where the vowels resonate.*

3.   *Practice and hold a pot on your head with both hands. This will keep your head still and open you up across your chest.*

4.   *Practice and swing your arms at the same time. This will really help to open up and relax your body.*

5.   *Rehearse using a mirror, observing your general body use and paying particular attention to how you are standing. Make sure you are open in your body and not slumped or hunched. Work out where you are going to look when you are making your presentation – remember, eye contact is very powerful.*

6.   *Work on your delivery. Make sure the pitch is varied and not on a monotone. This is so important as it will help to bring your presentation to life. Listen to how newsreaders and presenters on television and radio do this.*

7.   *You need energy in your delivery. You will have more control over this as you develop control of your breath.*

8.   *Practice using visualization techniques (see page 139).*

Rehearsal Technique

Many singers damage their voices by overdoing things in rehearsal. Be sensible and don't over-sing and tire out your voice. If you are singing with a choir, obviously it is not up to you when to take breaks, but don't sing at full throttle for the whole rehearsal. Often a rehearsal will be two to three hours long and your voice will get tired if you are not careful.

If you are rehearsing with a band you have more control. However, the rehearsal studio is a danger zone for a lot of singers. Don't sing all the time you are rehearsing. Pace yourself and take decent breaks. Don't sing constantly at full volume. Clearly, you want to build up your strength, but don't push it.

Classical singers, in rehearsals, protect their voices by 'marking'. This means that they don't sing out fully. For example, they may sing high passages either quietly or an octave down. They do as much as they feel is right at the time, depending how close they are to their performance.

You might consider doing something similar yourself. If you have got a lot of high material, sing it in your head voice or falsetto, down an octave, or take a lower harmony. Never push the top. If your voice starts to feel tired, stop singing. Also, if the rehearsal is going well and your voice feels good, don't be tempted to keep going until your voice packs up.

A guy I used to teach cancelled his lesson one day as he had overdone it during a rehearsal. I was quite surprised because he was particularly focused, practiced hard and was developing a good technique. I asked him what had happened and he explained that he was singing so well and enjoying himself so much that he got carried away. He was fine for the first five hours, but it was the next three that did him in! I had to laugh.

If you can't hear yourself properly you may well start to 'push' the sound and this will put pressure on your vocal cords. Some people use headphones and earplugs, or 'inner ears' but the best way of hearing yourself is to get the rest of the band to turn down. They may take some persuading, but it is for everyone's benefit in the end.

Tour And Gig Survival

If you want to survive regular gigging, touring, long recording stints or a heavy rehearsal schedule, you need to know how to look after your voice properly (this goes for both lead and backing vocalists). Everything I have said so far about taking care of your voice is relevant.

If you misuse your voice through constantly straining and tightening your throat area, your vocal cords can become swollen and will not meet properly. This will result in the sound becoming very breathy or hoarse. More seriously, if this keeps occurring it may result in long-term damage and eventually the dreaded nodules.

As I have said, most strained voices will recover with rest, which isn't much help if you are in the middle of a tour or recording an album. However, there is a lot you can do to avoid straining your voice in the first place.

Using the breath properly to support your singing is crucial. You need to work the breath and not your throat muscles. Having a good singing technique is the single most important factor in preserving your voice, but consider following a number of basic dos and don'ts.

I have already given you some practical advice on voice care and in the section on *Gigging Sound* we have covered issues relating to monitors, sound and sound people. If, despite everyone's best efforts you still end up not hearing yourself well, try your hardest not to push. It won't help the audience hear any better, and in all likelihood will result in you straining your voice. Change to using your head voice or falsetto more if you are having problems with high stuff.

Drink lots of water (but not iced water or alcohol) before a gig. You should try not to cough or clear your throat too vigorously (it is too abrasive on the cords). In fact, if you have a bad cold or sore throat try not to sing – you run the risk of losing your voice for a long period.

DON'T SMOKE! DON'T SMOKE! DON'T SMOKE!

Eating immediately before a gig is not recommended. As we have seen, many singers avoid certain types of food such as dairy products like cheese or chocolate as they find these create too much mucus.

It is all very well, I hear you say, telling us to avoid noisy, smoky boozy atmospheres, when that is exactly what we would normally expect from the average rock venue. I know, but I am just suggesting you avoid what you can. It is easy, for example, after a gig with the adrenalin still pumping, to slip into a lot of high-spirited shouting. But you could just as easily train yourself to chill-out after a gig and not do this, thereby protecting your voice. Remember, if you are talking in a noisy place, make your voice nasal.

For one reason or another, people *do* strain their voices and the level of physical difficulty or damage this can present varies.

Breakdown And Recovery

If you have persistent voice problems, your GP/physician will generally refer you to a voice specialist who will assess the nature of the damage and may take a look at your vocal cords with the help of a laryngoscope. This is a little camera on the end of a probe fed in through your nose (yuk!). You may have a general soreness, or some sort of swelling on your cords caused by misuse. This swelling could turn out to be a cyst, a polyp or a nodule.

Incidentally, one famous singer I worked with was unlucky enough to have a cyst *inside* one of his cords, which is quite rare (and in this case, it seems likely he was born with it). He had it removed by surgery and has worked hard to build a good singing technique. Ironically, I think it is the best thing that could have happened to him, as he has had to learn to take care of his voice and use it properly. In my opinion, he is now singing better than he has ever done.

Nodules

Nodules are the most common lesions that can develop on your vocal cords (folds). They are very rarely larger than 1.5 mm in diameter and are non-malignant. They are a bit like calluses and are formed by trauma arising from contact between opposite surfaces of the vocal cords. They are usually symmetrical, with one on each cord. Very occasionally sufferers will just have one.

There is still some debate about whether surgery is the best solution, but the trend is increasingly away from this. Generally these days, nodules are treated (and eliminated) using a combination of speech therapy and, if you are a singer, good singing lessons. The success rate is now quite high – so if you *are* unfortunate enough to have nodules, don't lose heart. If you have avoided them so far, follow the advice above and keep it that way.

The difficulty with voice disorders is that you can get into a vicious circle with them. Often it can start with laryngitis, a bad cough, or an infection resulting in lots of throat-clearing. All these things can leave your vocal cords sore and swollen. If you then sing, your poor cords don't stand a chance. The best advice is not to sing if you have got a bad cold or sore throat as you risk permanent damage.

Of course many problems arise purely as a result of poor voice use, including excessive shouting at sports games or over loud music, and 'pushing' your voice in a harmful way when singing. As you begin to experience vocal problems you will often have to push or force more to get the sound out. This makes the problem even worse, which is why it is crucial to spot difficulties early on and deal with them.

I have worked with many singers who either have or have had nodules. I usually know when someone has nodules, even before they tell me – and before they know themselves in some cases. There are a number of telltale signs (however, these symptoms on their own are not always definitive evidence of the existence of nodules): as a rule, a singer with nodules will find that their voice is particularly husky in the mornings and take a long time to warm up. Some people's voices will be permanently husky. For some time they may have felt a general soreness for a while after strenuous voice use.

If you have always sung in tune and then begin to experience problems with pitching notes, this can be an indicator as well. You may find your voice has become lower in pitch. This is a result of the increased mass of the vocal cords, which will vibrate at a lower frequency than usual.

Nodules can also make you produce a very breathy tone due to the fact that your vocal cords won't meet properly, allowing extra air to escape with the sound. It can be so breathy and weak in the upper middle part of your voice that the sound almost disappears.

Another common problem associated with nodules is the inability to sing at medium volumes: you may find you can sing only at the extremes (very quietly or at full belt) and that nothing much happens in between.

Some people have just one or two of the above symptoms; others display pretty much all of them.

If you are experiencing any of these problems on a frequent basis I suggest you get referred to a voice specialist. Only an expert can tell you exactly what is causing your problems – the symptoms I have described may be no real cause for concern, but could be evidence of various forms of voice disorder.

It is only if your nodules harden that you will have to have surgery. It is preferable to avoid surgery if at all possible since you will end up with scar tissue on your cords. This may well affect your singing, as your cords are unlikely to meet in the same way they did before.

It is essential that you learn to look after yourself properly if you have had nodules (or any other voice disorder), whether you have had surgery or not, because if you continue with the same pattern of abuse they may recur.

The section on voice care will help you learn to look after your voice properly. If you keep your voice healthy and develop a good singing technique, this will ensure that you avoid vocal problems, leaving you free to enjoy a long life of singing.

I don't want to frighten you, though. The most severe problems are rare and it is easy to become paranoid every time you get a sore throat. If you learn to use your voice healthily you can be pretty sure you will avoid any nasties!

On The Mend

Speech therapists tackle all types of voice disorder. Much of their work is with professional voice users, such as public speakers, actors, teachers, presenters, telephone-users, and, of course, singers.

They start by teaching good vocal hygiene, which I have been through elsewhere in this book.

Sometimes complete voice rest is recommended for certain problems, but, as I keep emphasizing, you must learn to use your voice properly if the symptoms are not to return.

A speech therapist will help you to develop a good general vocal technique – normally focusing on the speaking voice. They teach many of the aspects of technique outlined in this book such as breathing and support, vowel formation and resonance, and good body use.

Getting it right obviously takes practice. It takes time to get your muscles working in the right way, especially if you have slipped into bad vocal habits. Learning to use your voice correctly may mean that you will never need another visit to the speech therapist.

Working Environment

Many working environments contribute towards voice strain. This is particularly true of jobs that demand excessive voice use, or those that require you constantly to raise your voice.

Passive smoking is another problem. Working in smoky atmospheres is not good for you or your voice. You may be in a smoky office (although this is becoming much rarer), or work in a bar or club where you cannot avoid inhaling smoke. I would recommend regular steaming if this is the case. Some singers I know have changed jobs because of such problems.

When I left university, in order to subsidize the (initially meagre!) income I got from singing, I did a telesales job for some time. I found the constant talking on the phone a real strain on my voice and this was starting to have an adverse affect on my singing. I was fortunate enough to have a sympathetic boss who agreed to let me move to the admin department instead.

CHAPTER 20 SUMMARY

- It is important to follow basic principles of voice care in order to keep your voice healthy and working well. See the Dos and Don'ts table on page 159.

- Many people are heavy voice users at work. Just like singers, these people will also benefit from learning about breath, support, resonance, openness and having a free body.

- Those having to give a talk or presentation may wish to prepare themselves using the suggestions given in this chapter.

- Rehearsing your material is very important, but guard against over-doing things since you will make your voice tired and run the risk of losing it.

- Those on long tours must take extra care with their voices. Having a good singing technique is the most important factor, but singers should also look after their voices in between gigs.

- Excessive voice misuse and strain can lead to a general soreness, or some sort of swelling on your cords. This swelling may turn out to be a cyst, a polyp or a nodule.

- Rest and the use of steam are the only real remedies for voice loss and swollen cords.

- Serious problems are not common and even nodules rarely require surgery these days.

- Nodules are now more commonly treated with a combination of good vocal hygiene, speech therapy, and, if you are a singer, good singing lessons.

- If you have had problems, you must learn to use your voice properly if the symptoms are not to return.

- If you are serious about your singing, you may have to consider changing aspects of your working environment.

Chapter 21
Warm-Up

There is a difference between practicing singing exercises and warming up.

The word *exercise* suggests a workout and that is what singing exercises are designed to do. They are for strengthening and gaining more control over your voice.

When you warm up your voice you are *not* doing a workout; you are simply warming it up in readiness to sing. Warm-ups are usually quite short: the last thing you want is to tire your voice out before you start.

Warming up your voice will take longer on some days than it does on others. It will all depend on how tired you are, if you have been drinking, had a late night, or spent time in a smoky atmosphere. If you have been overdoing things vocally, your voice will also feel harder to start up.

It is advisable to get your voice going a few hours before you sing. If your voice is not feeling great you could start by having a steam before warming up. However, you don't need to do your warm-up all in one go.

Pavarotti, the master of singing technique, warms up in short bursts on the day of a performance. You will like this bit: he sleeps in until about 11 or 12 o'clock. When he wakes up he sings immediately for a few minutes. After breakfast he then sings for about fifteen minutes. He has another burst of five minutes before he goes to the venue and another five minutes before he goes on stage.

Why Do A Warm-up?

If you were going to play sport, go for a run or do a dance class, you would always do some sort of warm-up or stretching beforehand, or, at least, at the beginning of a session. When you are taking part in sport, you are often using muscles in ways they are not normally used. Stretching and loosening up will reduce the likelihood of damage, and also help to maximize your performance. Singing involves specific muscle use and so a warm-up has the same importance.

Warming up does what it says. Your voice will feel smoother, more open and resonant, more flexible and probably louder. If you never warm up before singing there is a risk of long-term damage.

Always warm up before you sing, whether it is for a choir or band rehearsal, gig or soundcheck. You need to make time for it, even if it has to be in the shower or in the car on the way to the venue. You run the risk of damaging your voice more easily if you sing 'cold'. Furthermore, your vocal performance is almost guaranteed to be poorer as a result.

I know for a fact that Tony Hadley, for example, religiously warms up his voice before every gig. It is no coincidence that he continues to maintain very high vocal standards after many years in the business. Those artists hoping for a long singing career will be wise to follow Tony's example – and that of many other long-standing artists, by doing the same.

As I have said, you don't need to do a long warm-up – about 5 or 10 minutes will do for most people. Don't make it an extensive vocal workout; if the warm-up becomes vocally tiring this is obviously counter-productive.

When you warm up you need to get your whole voice going. Obviously, there are many different ways of doing this – one would be to base your warm-up around your favorite singing exercises.

A simple warm-up would run something like this:

Start with some gentle humming using one of your simplest exercises. Then sing the same thing on an 'oo', and then an 'ee', or 'oh' and 'ah' if you prefer. Don't take it too high – concentrate on feeling the resonance.

Now sing a few fast arpeggios or articulation exercises. These will get your head voice going.

Move on to some slower exercises – maybe going up and down a major triad. Start in the middle of your voice and take it down in semitones, so it feels nice and open in your chest.

Next sing the first five notes of a major scale up and down slowly in the middle part of your voice.

You could then sing through a few phrases of one of your songs firstly on an 'ee' then an 'ah' and finally with the words.

Warm-up Exercises

You can warm up your voice in a number of different ways. You could select some of your favorite singing exercises from the ones I have given you, but be careful not to push. You should aim to get your voice open, connected to the support, and resonating.

If the exercises don't suit you, try other warm-ups. If you are warming up your voice for speech or singing, the following are all good.

This first one is a favourite of mine:

1. Hang down to the floor like a rag doll, with either straight legs or knees slightly bent – whatever is comfortable. Let your head and arms hang and your neck be free. Breathe in and out through your nose. Hum a single note, fairly low in your voice – wherever it feels good. The note will last for as long as the breath lasts. Feel it resonating in your back. Repeat five times.

2. Put your hands on your waist, bring your head up so that it is in line with your spine, breathe in and come up to standing. Let your arms hang loosely by your sides and repeat the humming, this time concentrating on the sound resonating in your chest. Do this five times.

3. Remain standing. Repeat the humming, imagining the resonance is coming into the front of your face around your sinuses. It may help to raise the pitch of the hum. (Rest your fingers lightly on the front of your face to feel the resonance.)

4. Stay standing. Place your hands on the back of your head. Repeat the humming thinking of the resonance buzzing in the back of your head.

> 5.   *Let your arms hang loosely by your sides. Now hum and imagine all these resonances joining up from the base of your spine, up your back, into the back of your head, over the top of your head, into the front of your face then chest, and down into your tummy.*

This is a great warm-up and one that really gets you in touch with the different areas in your body where you can resonate the sound. If you do this with your eyes closed it will be more powerful.

Singing long, held notes on any vowel you like is another good warm-up. Choose mid-range to low notes.

Another excellent warm-up technique is 'sirening'. This is a hum on an 'ng' sound rather than an 'mm'. You produce the sound right at the front of your face, behind your nose. You need to open your mouth as you go higher. Sirening encourages a good jaw position (but be careful not to tense your tongue).

> *Start at the bottom of your voice and slide right up to the top as high as you can go, and then all the way down. You can also try going from high to low. You will sound a bit like a cat or a siren (and indeed some unkind people may say that's how you usually sound). The idea is to do this completely smoothly with no gear changes, which can be quite tricky. Being able to achieve this is a sign of a healthy voice.*

Always keep a check to make sure your body isn't tense when you are warming up, or doing exercise. You could try some arm swinging or some of the other body-freeing exercises.

> *A good warm-up to get your lips, teeth and tongue going is to say the words 'chocolate' and 'minim'. Walk around the room swinging your arms saying 'chocolate' (clearly emphasizing each syllable) as many times as you can in one breath. Vary the pitch of it, going higher and lower. Repeat this several times. Then do the same on the word 'minim'. This makes the front of your mouth, lips, teeth and tongue more 'alive' and ready for action.*

Chapter 22
Singing Lessons

Do I Need Singing Lessons?

This is a very good question. Obviously I would say yes – but it depends from whom! Undoubtedly, everyone can benefit from good vocal tuition, but there are I am afraid, a lot of vocal coaches out there whose teaching you need like a hole in the head. Bad singing teaching can range from downright useless to actively damaging. But before I get on my high horse about those responsible, let's talk about the positive effects of good singing coaching.

All types of people come to me for lessons, from top professionals wishing to hone their skills, to people who sing purely for fun and are curious about their own potential. Many people use it as a form of therapy as they can really lose themselves in their singing.

Singing undoubtedly does have a beneficial effect, at both a physical and emotional level. Put simply, it makes you feel better!

Obviously, different people will want to take their singing onto different levels. You may want to be able to sing purely for your own personal enjoyment, perform a song at a party, play a leading role in your local operatic company, or front a rock band. Whatever your aspirations, good singing lessons can help you achieve it.

It is exciting when you start to explore your voice. I view working on singing as a journey. I love the fact that everybody's voice is different. I get a buzz from hearing someone's voice for the first time and working out exactly what they need to do to improve their singing.

Some people have lessons to prove to themselves that they can actually hold a tune. These tend to be adults who at an early age were told they couldn't sing. As I said earlier, everyone can learn to sing in tune given time. I haven't had a failure yet! It gives people such a feeling of happiness and satisfaction to be able to achieve what they and others always believed impossible. To learn to sing in tune is a surprisingly important and significant issue for many people.

Some people have lessons if they are preparing for an audition. Others may have joined a drama group and need to get their confidence up.

Some singers, sadly, only come when they are experiencing difficulties. Maybe they have started singing with a band and are struggling in rehearsals.

Very experienced singers also have lessons to keep on top of their technique and to make sure that their voices stay in good shape. It doesn't matter how good you are; it is easy to get a bit sloppy and fall into bad habits. It can be very useful to have someone else's 'ears' listening to you, checking that everything is okay and looking for areas that can be improved. Others can often hear things about your singing that you don't hear yourself.

You can never stop learning and improving. I am still learning new things all the time about singing and I want it to stay that way!

What Happens In A Singing Lesson?

Singing lessons vary and every teacher will have a different style and slightly different emphasis.

In a typical lesson I would cover breathing and voice exercises as well as working on a song. The exercises would take up more or less the first half of the lesson. When working on the song I would make sure that the singer was singing it technically as well as possible, focusing on breath, support, resonance, use of registers and good body use. I would also work on interpretation, style and phrasing.

However, if someone was working on a piece for a performance, audition or recording that week, I would do a short warm-up and spend more time on the song or songs.

Some teachers are great technicians and spend the majority of their lessons on technique and not much on repertoire. I personally like to do both.

Some singing coaches only deal with interpretation and phrasing and don't do any work on sound production and technique. Such coaches tend to be excellent pianists. Many classical singers use these, in addition to their singing lessons, to help them to learn repertoire.

When learning repertoire thoroughly you need to practice with the appropriate accompaniment. If you are preparing for an audition or recital, a few sessions with a good accompanist/coach is a great way of rehearsing.

How Do You Know You've Got A Good Teacher?

I strongly believe in a singer having a solid vocal technique. A good teacher should have a thorough knowledge of how the voice works and be able to convey it in simple, understandable language. I also believe they should be experienced singers themselves.

As a general rule, never be bullied into doing anything in a lesson that makes your voice feel very uncomfortable or results in your developing a sore throat. Sometimes when you are working on technique, you may be focusing on loosening your tongue or jaw, for example, and you may experience some tension or tightness in that area. If this happens, discuss it with your teacher – don't keep quiet.

Your teacher should be able to give you things to prevent this from happening. If not, they should stop that particular exercise and try something different. If your voice is repeatedly getting sore or tired in your lessons, frankly, you should change teachers.

Sometimes your voice may get tired when you are practicing or having a lesson due to the material you are singing. Some singers insist on singing material that is too high or 'pushy' for them. Certainly, through practice, you can develop strong support and it will become much easier to sing higher without straining.

I have taught plenty of rock singers who, after several months of hard work, were able to do their rehearsals and gigs without vocal strain. You need to start gradually and build up. Don't sing too high for too long, as you will get vocally tired.

Frequently, when singers start working on their technique they find they can keep it going for a while, but then their support muscles stop working. Furthermore, the more they sing; the more the old tensions have a tendency of creeping back in. The idea then, is to work on material in short bursts and gradually build up stamina.

Personality is important. You need to get on with your teacher and have some sort of rapport. This doesn't mean you have to be best friends, but you certainly need to feel at ease with them.

Bad Teachers

Unfortunately there are many singing teachers out there who are not merely ineffective; they are, through the things they teach, actively causing damage to people's voices. I myself have been on the receiving end of several such teachers over the years and feel very strongly about the subject.

My first complaint against the poorest teachers I encountered is that they had an inability to hear where I had technical difficulties. Secondly, they forced me to do things with my voice it really didn't want to do.

I think as a singer you should trust your instincts. If you are given something to do that doesn't feel right then don't do it. I appreciate this is not always as easy as it sounds: you tend to trust your teacher, and it can be hard to question their authority.

In my case, I was very focused and therefore practiced very hard. Sadly, this just reinforced the bad practices that I was taught and made things even worse. I look back on this now and know that at the time I felt quite uneasy about some of the things I was asked to do. But as I was, and still am, passionate about singing I practiced hard – very hard. The trouble was that I was practicing totally the wrong kinds of things.

The only good thing about having experienced so much bad teaching is that I had to work through this in order to gain a thorough understanding of what comprises good practice. I am sure, as a result, it has made me a better teacher.

I have collected a number of horror stories regarding singing teachers over the years. Some derive from personal experience and others have been told to me by singers with whom I have worked.

I know of one well-known teacher of rock and pop singers, for example, who starts by putting on a recording of a singer doing vocal exercises. The poor student is then expected to sing along. If a teacher does this they have very little control over what the singer is doing. There is so much potential for damage.

It is vital that the exercises are tailored to individual needs since no two singers are the same. I constantly stop during exercises to draw attention to different aspects of technique – vowel formation, breath, support, resonance, placing, registers, etc.

This particular teacher gives little or no instruction as to how to do the exercises and doesn't stop the 'backing' if the exercises are too high or out of range. He has even been known to flick through his filofax while the poor singer is struggling their way though the exercises! Appalling.

As I have already mentioned, occasionally singers are taught to sing their material exclusively using a mic. Sure, practicing with a mic has its place, but if you only ever sing like this you will never develop any depth in your voice or decent technique. You will be left with a shallow voice that lacks resonance, tone and support.

Classical singing teachers don't escape unscathed. Most will have studied singing extensively, but many don't have a sound knowledge of technique or the mechanics of the voice.

Just because you are a good singer it doesn't automatically follow that you will be a good teacher. Many are just plain ineffective, neither good nor bad, but others will really do damage. All my teachers were classical singers and I have been taught many weird and wonderful things. One teacher used a technique that involved almost 'shouting' the notes as high as I possibly could. The idea was to get you in touch with your emotional centre and place the voice where you speak – nightmare! It always hurt and she often reduced me to tears in the lesson.

Another teacher I had at university totally failed to hear that I wasn't singing with enough upper resonance and that I was really pushing the top of my voice. I was singing very high repertoire at the time and I had a huge amount of tension in my jaw – in fact, it used to seize up as I was singing! She did nothing to help me. My breath control became hopeless as I always forced the sound. The only thing that saved me was that my degree course finished and I didn't have to study with her any more.

'Excessive talking' is another problem among some teachers. Now, I like a good chat myself, but I build this into my schedule as 'spill-over' time. Unfortunately some teachers don't. These people like the sound of their own voices. They can spend virtually the whole lesson sharing stories about who they have taught and what they have done and end up doing very little teaching. I know a very well-known teacher of West End show singers who can spend as much as 45 minutes of a one-hour lesson talking, and leave only 15 minutes for teaching! Well, if you find that acceptable, that is up to you. I wouldn't put up with it myself, especially as some of these charlatans are charging a fortune!

Avoid teachers who appear to adopt what feels like a negative approach to your singing. One teacher, after listening to me sing for the first time said, rather disparagingly, 'Well, I suppose your voice is *usable*'! I was at the time working as a professional singer. I may have had a few minor technical problems, but people always seemed to like the sound I made. Fortunately, I had a strong self-image and swiftly moved on to another teacher. I don't know what her problem was, or if she knew anything about technique – I suspect not – but it could have put me off for life!

I strongly believe in taking a positive approach and use a lot of encouragement and praise. There is never any excuse for being unkind or patronizing – or sycophantic for that matter. Interestingly, there are some artists who will always go to singing coaches who have mastered the art of ego massage, regardless of how useless they might be from a technical point of view. I know of some successful 'media' singing coaches who are excellent at this, but if you scratch beneath the surface, you will find only a very patchy knowledge of technique.

The proof of the pudding, as they say, is in the eating. If a singing coach is worth their salt (assuming you have a willing singer) then you should see a marked improvement in the singing pretty quickly. The history of singing coaching has always been marked by accusations (often justified) of charlatanism. I say, if you are doing everything your singing coach is telling you to do and practicing conscientiously, but you still don't experience any obvious progress, then it's time you change your singing coach.

Finally, be suspicious of people who say they don't take beginners. It is usually because they don't know enough about technique and wouldn't know where to start. I find myself questioning the motivation of these people in becoming singing teachers in the first place. As far as I'm concerned, if someone is keen to work on their voice then I am too, whatever level they are at. I love the challenge of different voices and the 'problem-solving' side of things – figuring out the areas that need to be worked on in order to get the absolute best out of their singing.

I enjoy my singing coaching and try always to achieve the highest possible standards. I love what I do and feel very lucky to earn my living this way. I have met a lot of wonderful people over the years through my work, many of whom have become close personal friends.

CHAPTER 21 SUMMARY

- You should always do some kind of warm-up before you sing.

- Like other kinds of physical activity, singing involves specific muscle use and so a warm-up has the same importance.

- A warm-up is not an extensive workout – 5 to 10 minutes are usually sufficient.

- Suggestions for ways of warming up are given in this section.

- Every singer can benefit from good vocal tuition, but caution should be exercised when choosing a singing teacher.

- The kinds of things to look for and those to avoid in a singing teacher are discussed in this section.

Afterword
My Top Ten Singers

I am often asked who my favourite singers are and why. It's a very tricky question to answer – like having to select your Desert Island Discs.

Because I like singers for all kinds of reasons, it makes bringing the choice down to ten almost impossible. One singer may have a great technique, or a particular tonal quality. Another's phrasing or delivery of lyrics may stand them apart. Some singers will captivate due to sheer musicality.

A Top Ten, by its very nature, is always going to be a personal, idiosyncratic thing and my choices won't be everyone's cup of tea. It might be interesting to analyse your own vocal Top 10 in this way – you often don't know why you like something until you take the time to think about it.

Luciano Pavarotti

Top of my list for flawless technique has to be Luciano Pavarotti. Whether or not you like opera singers, you have to admire his control and power. Even if you never listen to opera, everyone knows his rendition of 'Nessun Dorma'. His voice is so even and balanced. He appears to sing with the whole of his body (and you have to admit, there's plenty of it!) and has an incredibly well-supported voice. When he soars away on his top Cs he keeps his head and body very still (he very definitely never pulls his head back, rock'n'roll style!); you can see him drawing everything in and down.

I also love the bright resonance in his voice – there is a real 'ring' to it. The placing of the sound is forward in his face and head, but he also has a very open throat, which adds so much power to his singing. You are aware of no obvious change in tone when he moves from chest to head voice. His 'passagio' (the transition area between chest and head voice) is so beautifully blended.

Pavarotti has made so many excellent recordings, but one album to check out is *King Of The High C's* if you want to hear some sparkling singing!

Stevie Wonder

Stevie Wonder is my next choice. He is another singer who is totally in command of his voice. There is so much power and emotion in his sound. His voice is a very flexible instrument. In fact, listen to his harmonica playing; it is so much like his singing. He bends notes and varies vibrato, constantly changing the 'color' of his singing. Above all else, he has such an uplifting, happy-sounding voice. His tone is very bright and you can virtually hear his smile in the sound. Think of the 'la, la, la' section in 'My Cherie Amour'; it is such a joyful, inspiring sound. The singing is always effortless and so well controlled. His phrasing and feel are superb and his vocals have so much excitement and energy, whilst retaining tremendous line. He is without doubt a singer who gets in the groove. He also has a very agile voice and is brilliant at scatting and doing really fast 'licks'.

Stevie has sung so many great songs such as 'Superstition', 'Signed, Sealed Delivered, I'm Yours', 'I Wish', ' You And I', 'You Are The Sunshine Of My Life', 'Lately' and the list goes on and on. I couldn't possibly just choose one.

Frank Sinatra

Frank Sinatra would be on most people's list. Apart from anything else, he is the supreme phraser. There are so many great songs associated with him: 'Chicago', 'New York, New York', 'The Lady Is A Tramp', 'Mack The Knife', 'Come Fly With Me' and of course 'My Way'. My absolute favorite has to be 'It Was A Very Good Year'. His singing of this is sublime. The meaning he puts into the words is almost tangible. The tone of his voice is rich and warm and his phrasing is out of this world. Not only does he have such a listenable tone and smooth delivery but his timing is pure genius. Although 'Old Blue Eyes' was a master of the classic ballad, clearly, this was a guy who also knew how to swing!

Eva Cassidy

For emotional intensity my vote has to go to Eva Cassidy. She had a golden voice and used so many different colours and textures when she sang. She could sing with a full tone and a lot of power or an intense fragility. She was completely at one with her instrument (acoustic guitar) when she played and I believe that may be at the root of her wonderful musicality. Her singing was spellbinding and she was someone who completely made a song her own. As far as I am concerned she brought a new meaning to the term 'cover version' and blew everybody else out of the water. There are not many people who can cover old classics successfully. Her version of 'Over The Rainbow' reduces me to tears every time.

Maria Callas

Someone else who sang with extraordinary emotion was Maria Callas. In my opinion she is unrivalled in the world of opera. She sang with such intense passion and drama, and drew out every last nuance of meaning in both the words and music. She used a wonderful variety of tone and colour and her voice was incredibly thrilling and moving. Her magnetic stage presence was legendary, but for those of us unlucky never to have seen her in the flesh, her recordings have certainly captured her magic.

She was a complete artist and supreme musician, famed for her complete devotion to her art. It is difficult to sum up in a few words what is so great about her singing. In fact, I think her singing is beyond words. One of my favourite recordings is of the aria 'Vissi d'arte' from Puccini's *Tosca* (La Scala, Milan 1953). The range of tone and expression she uses is quite breathtaking. She varies the weight of her voice and musical line to add to the drama. Pure genius!

Cecilia Bartoli

I love the Italian soprano Cecilia Bartoli for different reasons. She is not the 'heavyweight' that Callas was but has very special qualities of her own. She has a fantastically agile voice and a beautiful tone. She sings with real musicality, vitality and emotion. Her singing draws you in as a listener – she is a real communicator and one who is truly in touch with her emotional 'centre' as she sings.

Even though her voice is obviously very well produced and she is technically brilliant, there is something very 'natural' and fresh about her singing. It is this quality that I personally find particularly appealing. Her mastery of coloratura singing is awesome, but one of my favourite recordings is not actually one where she shows off her vocal pyrotechnics. 'Giusto ciel, in tal periglio' (Maometto II) from her recording of *Rossini Heroines* moves me with its beautiful line, simplicity and the degree of emotion.

Ella Fitzgerald

Ella Fitzgerald is another on my all-time-greats list. She is well known as one of the great jazz scatters. Her voice had tremendous agility and could really soar. It is, however, her recordings with the guitarist Joe Pass that have a very special place in my affections. When they played together, there was an almost symbiotic relationship – with one playing off the other. They produced a beautifully intimate sound, and I think the semi-acoustic guitar is a great vehicle for the voice. Their recording of the Billy Strayhorn classic 'Lush Life' is one of my all time favourites. Again, Ella's tone is so silky smooth and her singing always sounds completely effortless.

Aretha Franklin

Aretha Franklin has to be one of the most exciting singers of all time. She is known by many as the 'Queen of Soul' and soul she certainly has – heaps of it. She has huge power in her voice and pushes it to its limits. There is great energy and commitment in her singing and the more you listen to her, the more the excitement builds up inside you.

Her tone is incredibly bright and ringing and there is a real intensity and focus in her singing. She is completely 'on it' in terms of phrasing. She can throw her voice around wherever she likes, often bending it and using it like an instrument. I love the energy of her classic hit 'Respect' and the great soulful feel of 'Natural Woman'.

Amy Lee

Amy Lee, singer with the American rock band Evanescence, might seem to some an odd choice for a top ten. I wanted, however, to include a rock and pop singer and her singing on the band's first album *Eternal* proves that a young singer can stand alongside the best of them. Her voice has a lovely purity of tone and and she sings with impressive vocal technique. Her use of a strong mixed register allows her voice to cut right across what is quite a heavy-sounding band. Amy's rendition of the song 'Hello' is as near a perfect vocal as you can get. Her breath control is astonishingly good and she sings with wonderful musical line. The way she carries you with her through the final climax of the song is spellbinding. Right at the end she dramatically changes from a strong mixed register to an incredibly moving and intimate head voice.

Take 6

This is a bit of a cheat as, clearly, there is more than one of them! The reason I have included them in my list of favourites is that they take *a cappella* singing to another level. Their arrangements and choice of harmonies are sublime. The way they phrase together, change dynamics and blend their voices is mind-blowing.

I know I've already mentioned the song 'Get Away Jordan' (from the album *Take Six*) but you just have to listen to it. I find it hard to believe that six singers can sing so well together. They truly use their voices as instruments, providing all their own percussion and bass parts with their voices alone. In places they sound like a brass section. If you want to feel instantly uplifted, give them a go.

Inevitably when you write any 'best of' list people will say, 'but what about him' and 'how could you leave her out'. As I said earlier, the examples above were almost picked out at random, but hopefully they highlight many different aspects of good singing.

If my list hadn't been limited to ten, I would definitely want to say something about (in alphabetical order!): Oleta Adams, Tim Buckley, Karen Carpenter, Caruso, Jose Carreras, Ray Charles, Kurt Cobain, Nat King Cole, Craig David, Placido Domingo, Nick Drake, Donald Fagen, Judy Garland, Marvyn Gaye, Billie Holiday, Mahalia Jackson, Mick Jagger, Tom Jones, Alicia Keys, John Lennon, Paul McCartney, Joni Mitchell, Roisin Murphy, Leontyne Price, Robert Plant, Bonnie Raitt, Otis Redding, Diana Ross, Sting, Bryn Terfyl, Tina Turner, Thom Yorke. But even then, of course, there would be scores of others.

And finally...

If you have always wanted to improve your singing, I hope this book has inspired you to do something about it. Follow the basic advice in these pages and keep working at the exercises. Be inspired, and don't give up and eventually you will find *your* voice.

Good luck!

www.jothompson.net

Further Reading

The Alexander Technique Workbook (Richard Brennan)
Element Books Ltd...
ISBN: 1 85230 346 8

Great Singers On Great Singing (Jerome Hines)
Limelight Editions, New York
ISBN: 0 87910 025 7

The Voice And Its Disorders (Greene and Mathieson)
Whurr Publishers Ltd.
ISBN: 1 86156 196 2

(It's Your Life, What Are You Going To Do With It?) Coach Yourself'
(Anthony M. Grant & Jane Greene)
Momentum
ISBN: 1 843 04013 1

Yoga For You (Tara Fraser)
Duncan Baird Publishers, London
ISBN: 1 904292 27 5

Glossary

A Cappella
Unaccompanied.

Alexander technique
A technique to re-coordinate the body and inhibit body misuse.

Baritone
Male voice type, weightier than tenor.
Range: 2nd G below middle C to high G sharp.

Bass
Lowest male voice type.
Range: 2nd F below middle C to F above middle C.

Bass baritone
A male voice with a voice quality lighter than a bass.
Range: Low F to high F sharp.

The belt
Pushing the chest voice very high.

The break
The point at which the chest voice can be pushed no higher and the sound changes to pure head voice (undesirable).

Cadenza
A brilliant passage for solo instrument or voice.

Castrato
A male singer castrated before reaching puberty.

Contralto
The lowest female voice type.
Range: D below middle C to 2nd B flat above middle C.

Countertenor
Classical male singer who sings using mainly falsetto.

Chest resonance
Vibration of the singing sound felt in the chest.

Clavicular breathing
Shallow breathing. Breath drawn into the area around the top of the chest and collarbones.

Covering
Modifying the vowel sounds as you sing higher. All vowels become more of a 'yawny' 'awe' sound, sung with an 'open throat'.

Diaphragm
A dome-shaped area of muscle that separates your heart and lungs from the rest of your insides. The main muscle involved in breathing.

Diaphragmatic breathing
Breathing that concentrates on the movement of the diaphragm as a means of control.

Dynamics
Variations in volume that musicians use for emotional or dramatic effect.

Falsetto
The highest part of a man's voice – the 'choirboy' part.

Forward resonance
Resonance produced at the front of the face and head.

The 'groove'
The small cavity on either side of your cheeks.

Head resonance
Vibration of the singing sound felt in your head.

Intercostal breathing
A pattern of breathing that concentrates on the intercostal muscles surrounding your ribcage.

Larynx
Voice box.

Legato
Smooth and connected.

Low larynx
Keeping the larynx in a low, relaxed position when singing.

Lip synching
Miming to a pre-recorded vocal track.

Marking
Not singing at full volume in rehearsal.

Mezzo soprano
A female singer whose voice is weightier than a soprano but lighter than a contralto.
Range: F below middle C to 2nd B above middle C.

Nodules
Small non-malignant lesions on the vocal cords.

Open throat
Singing with an open 'yawny' space in the back of your throat.

Perfect pitch
The ability to recognise or name a note on first hearing.

Pharynx
The back wall of the throat.

Register
The range of a voice or an instrument.

Relative pitch
The ability to pitch notes from a given starting note.

Resonance
The amplification and alteration of the basic vocal sound by certain areas of the body.

Sight singing
The ability to sing music from a printed score without having previously rehearsed it.

Soft palate
The soft part at the back of the roof of your mouth.

Soprano
Highest female voice type.
Range: G below middle C up to high C (and beyond).

Support
The control of the breath as you sing.

Tenor
Highest male voice type.
Range: C below middle C to C above middle C.

Tessitura
A term used to describe the range of a voice or piece of music in relation to the normal range. If a song were said to have a high *tessitura*, most notes would lie quite high.

Trachea
Windpipe.

Vibrato
The vibration of the singing sound.

Vocal cords/folds
Two pieces of delicate elastic tissue reaching from the back to the front of the larynx.

Also available from Artemis Editions

'Handel's Messiah From Scratch' is a new, state-of-the-art, four-volume edition of this perennially popular choral work, comprising separate books for each voice part, each packaged with 2 CDs.

The first CD features a superb professional recording of all the choruses from Messiah, performed by an exceptional orchestra and chorus specially assembled from the UK's best musicians.

These unique recordings have the relevant voice part (e.g. the Soprano voice line in the Soprano edition) subtly increased in volume, bringing the part to the fore without disrupting the overall balance. The second CD includes a selection of warm-ups and specially designed exercises for every chorus.

'The most worthwhile publishing venture I've seen.' Natalie Wheen, *Classic FM*

'Music Makes Your Child Smarter' reveals the secret power of music in your child's development.

The first half of the book is an introduction to the many benefits of music on children's development, while the second half provides a simple guide for parents, arranged by age group, on how to introduce music into their child's life. Packed with games and activities, the book requires no musical knowledge and is illustrated throughout.

The book comes complete with a 53-track, 73-minute CD containing a huge variety of tracks for listening, demonstrations of the various activities and games, and other pieces designed to complement the advice in the book.

Endorsed by both the Royal Academy of Music and the Academy of St. Martin In The Fields, this book is a must-have for parents (whether musical or not), teachers and music educators.

"A fantastic self-help guide for parents – I very strongly recommend it to everyone." Sarah Stacey, *The Mail on Sunday*

View sample pages, listen to sample MP3s and buy at:

www.artemismusicshop.com

'Find Your Voice' Vocal Exercise CDs

NOW AVAILABLE – exclusive CDs of vocal exercises specially designed by author Jo Thompson to accompany this book.

Available in two versions (one for men and one for women), each audio CD contains 20 of Jo's favourite singing exercises. Each exercise is introduced with hints and tips by Jo and is demonstrated in full on the CD. Piano accompaniment tracks are also included for you to practise along with.

Each 47-track CD includes:
- Introduction and hints on each exercise by Jo Thompson
- Full demonstration of every exercise
- Piano backing tracks to practise along with
- MIDI files for every exercise

The MIDI files included on the CD allow you, with the aid of appropriate software, to transpose each exercise into a convenient key for your voice, and to speed up or slow down the exercise as required.

Only £9.99 each (inc. VAT)

Each CD includes
- How to use singing exercises
- Scales and arpeggios
- Legato and staccato exercises
- Stamina-building exercises
- Falsetto exercises (Male CD only)
- Practice hints and tips

Hear sample MP3s and buy exclusively from
www.artemismusicshop.com

Artemis | **EDITIONS**